# THE INVISIBLE WAR

## Pursuing Self-Interests at Work

# THE INVISIBLE WAR

## Pursuing Self-Interests
## at Work

**SAMUEL A. CULBERT**
**JOHN J. MCDONOUGH**
*University of*
*California*

*JOHN WILEY & SONS*
*New York Chichester*
*Brisbane Toronto*

*Library of Congress Cataloging in Publication Data*

Culbert, Samuel A
    The invisible war.

    Includes index.
    1.  Organizational behavior.  2.  Organization.
I.  McDonough, John Joseph, 1937-    joint author.
II.  Title.

HD58.7.C84      658.4      79-18682
ISBN 0-471-05855-6

Printed in the United States of America

10 9 8 7 6 5 4

With love
—to Gar
Samantha
Ann-Marie
John
and Elaine

# PREFACE

We wrote this book because we're alarmed and
have definite ideas about what should be different.
We're alarmed when we think about the bright
young people we teach in UCLA's Masters of Business Administration program and what they face
when going to work in today's institutions. We're
alarmed at the situations we find managers in as
they buy into strife and pressure in jobs which by

conventional standards are choice, but which we wouldn't want our kids to touch with a 50-foot pole. In fact, we despair when we think about the jobs that are going to be available when our children reach the job market. Think about it for a moment. How many jobs that you know of would you wish on someone you love? How do you warn a young person with a new degree going out with enthusiasm and self-confidence to join the ranks of a large corporation? What do you say to clients and associates you've gotten to know and like about the rat race they've chosen, when they genuinely don't see the negatives that occur to you?

*The Invisible War* is about the ways people must position themselves to do their work effectively and the battles they have to fight in order to get what they produce valued. People try to do their job in the way they can do it best while packaging in as many self-beneficial pursuits as they can get away with. And the specific way a person decides to do his or her job in turn determines how that person sees and interprets each organizational event—and our book describes why.

The issues taken up in this book are complex and do not lend themselves to simple prescriptions or a how-to-get-yours-at-the-other-guy's-expense treatment. We wince when promoters use exclamations like, "This book will make you a winner." Although, for ease of comprehension, we use plain words and have included many concrete illustrations, *The Invisible War* requires self-reflection and real human consideration. In the short run, it will help with many practical problems such as getting today's contributions valued while not stepping on the egos of those working around you. In the long run, it will help in seeing alternatives to the brutality that comes from self-convenient constructions of the truth, and will help you in establishing new patterns of asserting leadership, new ways of being powerful, and new formats for socializing others.

One self-indulgence, and we say this out loud because we view our readers as essential to making this effort a success. This book contains a unique slant on organization life which we believe can make a difference. It represents our wholehearted attempt to influence the world of work and make it suitable for the kind, generous, and sensitive people you respect and love.

Los Angeles, California                    Samuel A. Culbert
                                           John J. McDonough

# ACKNOWLEDGMENTS

Ask anyone who has attempted a serious book about people in organizations and they'll tell you it was a very tough book to write. There are so many realities with which to contend that formulating a coherent perspective rattles emotions as well as the brain. This book was four years in the making, and its completion is testimony to the help and support we received. Our friends really came through for us.

Stan Hinckley and Mort Lachman made invaluable contributions. Stan helped with our collaboration. He got involved at a time when we couldn't decide whether our difficulties were due to an illusive concept, a gap in our theory, or a hopelessly dense partner. Because Stan hung in, we eventually found our common structure. Now when someone asks "Who wrote what?" we point at one another and reply "He wrote every other word."

Mort Lachman was always available. We could find him when his secretary could not. He contributed everything from advice to an agent. But best of all he patiently read our false starts and was willing to say, "It's still terrible" at moments when everyone else was saying "It's wonderful."

We received editorial help from Debbie Silverman and Gaylin Rezek. Gaylin began with us, but the lengthiness of our project outlasted her availability. While with us, she gave laser-like attention to our every word and was quite generous with her involvement.

Debbie picked up as we hit our stride. Her special brand of sharpness and perspective was just what we needed. Not only did she help with details, but she contributed significantly to the flow that holds our chapters together. She found flexibility in a personal schedule that was every bit as busy as ours, and for that we will always be in her debt.

Many others also pitched in, but we fear that nam-ing them all will leave us with too little of the credit. Seriously, we are grateful to those who debated with us, counselled and cheered for us, and whose involvements kept us from settling for less than what this book has become. To Larry Lodico, Terence Krell, Bob Tannenbaum, Janet Richmond, Joel Gotler, Allen Koplin, Sy Goldstone, Chris Argyris, Herb Kindler, Rex Mitchell, Susan Nero, Len Zweig, Jerry Jeffers, Jim Jackson, Warren Bennis, and John Buckley, we extend our thanks and deep-felt appreciation.

S.A.C.
J.J.McD.

# CONTENTS

# THE INVISIBLE WAR

## Pursuing Self-Interests at Work

# THE
# INVISIBLE
# WAR

I

Each day we march off to an invisible war. We fight battles we don't know we're in, we seldom understand what we're fighting for, and worst of all, some of our best friends turn out to be the enemy. Our average workday consists of going to the office, sitting in meetings, speaking on the telephone— just talking to people. Yet we limp home physically battered and mentally anguished. It's like being attacked by a neutron bomb—the buildings are intact, but the people are decimated.

This is a book about modern organizations and the covert battles that take place as people pursue their self-interests in the name of organizational effectiveness. It describes the origins of these battles, their form, and, most of all, their cost to the individual and to the organization. In recent years these battles have been referred to as "games." But the word "game" implies a mental attitude that has, at its root, a sense of fair play and calls to mind victors who really win. Besides, the word "game" grossly understates the life-and-death stakes involved.

This book is written with everyone who works in an organization in mind. Our goals are simple. We want to make the conflict more visible, and we want to show well-intentioned people how self-interests can be pursued without brutality, while contributing to the organization's cause. We don't offer packaged solutions and instant cures. What we do offer is a new perspective on the inevitable fact that people are always looking for ways to pursue their self-interests. We seek to help readers avoid the conflict and create a more meaningful existence at work.

Our perspective is presented in four distinct sections. Part I reveals the nature of the war. It introduces the pervasiveness of self-interests and the duplicity that results from the need to keep self-interests hidden.

Part II depicts the stakes and the struggle. It describes specifically what people are fighting for and how they promote their self-interests while camouflaging their motives. We explain why people with the same job perform their work differently and why people with different jobs but the same objectives must fight interminably over whose way is best when a little effort behind any thoughtful approach would bring instant success to the organization.

Part III analyzes the tactics people use to survive these battles, the human pain these tactics cause, and the tragic inefficiency that results. We explain why a three-minute decision requires a four-hour meeting and why an innocent side-comment provokes a migraine headache.

Part IV tells how to de-escalate the war. It shows how people with diverse interests can work collaboratively for the greater organizational good. It presents alternatives to the destructive tactics used today. The carnage is not a necessity—there are ways not only to survive, but to prosper in the organizational no-man's land.

# 1 | SELF-INTERESTS AT WORK

A funny thing happened the other day. A member of the California State Legislature revealed how his self-interests affected his organizational decisions and, as a result, even his best friends ran for cover.

A reporter had asked State Assemblyman Jim Keysor why he had decided to run for the Los Angeles City Council. Wasn't that a step down in office? Assemblyman Keysor replied, "On the L.A. City Council I'd be working with 14 other councilmen at a salary of $33,000 annually. Right now, I'm working with an assembly of 80 members, 120 if you include senators, for an annual salary of $23,000. I'd be making one-third more as city councilman, people should understand that."* He gave other reasons as well. He said he was envious of the greater amount of publicity the news media gave local politicians, acknowledged that the City Council would be a better base from which to run for higher office, and said he thought his current position in the state legislature would scare off other candidates, letting him "steal the seat" in April. He also mentioned all the lofty missions of service and contribution a candidate mentions when making an appeal for voter support.

———◆———

It struck us as ironic that in this flagrantly atypical statement, this candidate was merely admitting the motivations that we suspect guide all candidates who run for public office, from dog catcher to president. In fact most of us would privately admit that Assemblyman Keysor was seeking little more than what all organization players pursue—a niche from which to exert influence and be personally expressive, to earn just compensation, and to advance a career. Everyone knows there is a self-interested side to each person's involvements—a side that determines which tasks get addressed and how each is accomplished. But in Assemblyman Keysor's case, being candid about the self-interests that dictated his involvements created a storm of protest. In fact, within days of this interview appearing in the press, he was forced to withdraw his candidacy and was burdened with repaying the "war chest" amassed for the campaign.

The lesson about the revelation of self-interests goes far beyond politics. Woe unto the people, in any arena, who reveal their personal stake in the organization decision at hand. Such revelations make it possible for others who think differently to portray one's actions as self-serving and to discredit

* L.A. Times, February 26, 1977.

his or her point of view. The organization world is confused by a false ethos of rationality which does not allow people to acknowledge the extent to which self convenience, temperament, and personal values play a role in determining how they and others see their jobs and decide to do them. That's why the smart guys keep their interests hidden. In fact, success in pursuing what's personally important rests in not tipping off that self-interests are involved.

At some level, of course, most people do recognize that personal needs and self-convenience dictate a good deal of what they and others do. But there's a bit of a double standard in how they react when these self-interests are brought to their attention. When people observe self-interests in their own actions they claim "happy coincidence." When they observe it in what others do, they are *inclined* to scream "exploitation." We say inclined because whether or not they scream depends on how their self-interests match up with the other person's "exploitation." When there's a good match they are less inclined to protest.

As long-time organization consultants and researchers, we've been studying self-interests for years. Initially we were intrigued with how clandestine people have to be about a force that is so central to their lives at work. In particular, we questioned the costs associated with a system in which people are primarily motivated by self-interests but in which success rests on an ability to portray oneself as concerned primarily with benefiting the organization. We understood that self-interests and personal needs are bootlegged into every aspect of the job, and we were concerned about the damage done by the underground way people are forced to express them. Accordingly, we decided to analyze and research the situation more carefully.

Our efforts proved enlightening. We discovered a perspective for viewing what most people sense but never quite accept. We could see considerable human and organizational costs in the way people pursue that which is personally important at work. Our first impulse was to expose and criticize these costs in Ralph Nader style. However, we feared that an exposé without a proposed instant cure would merely result in more strenuous attempts at concealment. Besides, there are alternatives even though they are not the simple cut-and-dried ones that practical management prefers. But this is not a simple problem. Hence the reason for this book.

---

To begin with, our research showed us that what people advocate—on what they claim are strictly rational and objective grounds—almost always appears quite different once their self-interests are shown. We found a system of operating that disconnects thoughts, words and deeds. People think one thing and say another. People say they are doing one thing while they are doing something else. What is said and done in one moment is often at odds with what is said and done in the next. And schisms like these can be seen in every organization and at each level. We saw them at Procter and Gamble, we saw them at Peat, Marwick, Mitchell, and we saw them at the PTA. We saw them on the shop floor, in middle management, and in the corporate board room.

We found that schisms in thought, word and deed are what allow professionals, from doctors to accountants, to push for self-serving rules and practices while casting themselves as the guardians of the public's welfare. We found that they underlie the type of moral decay that took place in the Nixon White House, that is taking place in the upper echelons of our nation's businesses, and that is a major cause of the increasing rigidity that characterizes labor's position in the modern industrial society. Moreover, we found schisms have an impact on the daily lives of people at work, corrupting bottom-line definitions of organizational effectiveness, making accurate communications impossible, and breeding distrust among people whose common objectives should make them the staunchest of allies.

Yet, as Assemblyman Keysor's experience demonstrated, a refusal to invoke these schisms can result in organizational suicide. They are the only means people have for succeeding in a system where self-interest must not be known. For example, consider how many times a friend of ours named Roy had to engage in schisms, misrepresent and shade the truth, in order to survive a work day with a modicum of success and personal dignity.

———————————

By most standards Roy is a winner. He makes $50,000 a year as a manufacturing manager in a company listed on the New York Exchange. At forty-six he's no longer young enough to be labeled a "real comer," but he is sufficiently young to rate a shot at plant manager or even something bigger at corporate headquarters.

On the day in question, Roy's morning starts out with a downtown 7 o'clock meeting with his boss Mr. Cantrell, the Division Manager, concerning a request by corporate headquarters for backup data on a "product run analysis" performed by Roy's department.

"We know we're still not coming in with what they want to hear," protests Roy, "but we think our report is convincing. Our analysis clearly shows that their way costs 15% more with no extra gain."

Cantrell responds, "They've got a lot committed in the other direction. Better give the big boys what they want; there's no use fighting them at this point. Besides, if we hold out they'll see us as disloyal."

Roy reluctantly concedes, reasoning Cantrell is looking out for himself. Besides, he figures that he took this one far enough to demonstrate his sincerity.

The drive back to the plant gives Roy some time to think

up a strategy for breaking the news to his staff. He doesn't want to give them the impression that he laid down in front of his boss, which, incidentally, is what he thinks Cantrell did with his. He finally decides the best approach is to himself attack the assumptions on which their analysis is based.

Back at the plant, Roy encounters Harry, the secretary of a task-force Roy chairs, who has been waiting nearly an hour for their regularly scheduled meeting. As he ushers Harry into his office, Roy searches for an acceptable excuse. Unfortunately, he'd used some variant of "I was working on something with a big boss" the last two times he'd kept Harry waiting.

He needn't have worried, however, because Harry needs a favor and wants to keep a friendly tone. Harry blurts out, "I've got a confession to make. I took your name in vain yesterday."

Roy asks, "How's that?"

Harry responds, "Jim Todd over at production control laid into me for leaving their item off the agenda for next week's meeting and I said it was because you asked me to, pending some additional documentation. You did mention something like that and I couldn't stand to have Jim catch me up once again."

"Sure, I'll help you out," Roy says, "but let's spend a minute getting our stories straight."

Just as they finish, the phone rings. Roy finds himself promising a young corporate staffer that he'll have his cost reduction analysis completed by the middle of the month. After hanging up, he calls in one of the section heads and says, "Phil, I need your help. I need some cost reduction facts pulled together quicker than hell. I know your staff is up to their necks with the inventory problem but this one is important."

Then Roy goes over with Phil the details of the request, careful to conceal the letter of instructions that would reveal that today's emergency was a two-month-old assignment. He needn't have bothered. Phil is already wired into the grapevine and knows he is being had.

This is a part of the job that Roy detests—receiving the young puppies that corporate headquarters sends around on assignments intended primarily for training but which dig up data that will be used later on to attack his division— with the fallout trickling down on him. Through the years Roy has learned to respond by waiting because at least half the requests eventually die on the vine. But the ones that don't create the emergencies that drive him and his staff into a frenzy as he obediently passes the requests down without divulging that they lack meaning.

Shortly before noon Roy gets a drop-in visit from Jack, the quality assurance manager, who is also a close friend and ally. Sitting on Roy's desk, Jack says, "I stopped by to report a favor I did for you."

Roy: "I could use one today."

Jack: "I'm on the team that selects the visiting committee to check out European operations and I think I sold them on you."

Roy: "Did it take much selling?"

Jack: "Not really. The big criticism was that you aren't up to speed on technology. I countered by saying that you may be technologically flat, but then our Europeans aren't all that hot either, and besides you really know how to look authoritative."

Roy winces but doesn't say anything—his best buddy had, in the process of doing him a favor, just conceded the "technical incompetence" label that has plagued him throughout his career, that he is at a loss to understand, and that he tries never to concede.

As the conversation switches to a lighter vein, in drifts Ben, the R & D manager, asking, "Are you guys ready for lunch?" Roy looks painfully over at Jack, who quickly responds, "Actually we're talking shop but you're welcome to walk out to the parking lot with us." Alone again with Jack, Roy says, "Thanks, I couldn't take that phony today. He's always talking like a Boy Scout about how his department and mine should link better, but it's all lip-service and boring as hell."

A chance encounter on the way out of the restaurant provides Roy with the answer to why last month's corporate-wide meeting, called by the vice-president of manufacturing, had been switched at the last minute to, of all places, Chicago and delayed two weeks.

An old family friend grabs Roy's arm and says, "Hey, I discovered that your company's manufacturing vice-president and I are related through our wives. I bumped into him at his brother-in-law's 50th birthday party in Chicago last month."

The news that the meeting had been switched so that the boss could attend a birthday party really galls Roy and keeps him angry into the midafternoon. Making that meeting had cost him his vacation deposit and had provoked two weeks of needling by his wife.

As Roy settles back at his desk, in comes his secretary to announce that Roy's section head meeting would have to be postponed that week. It then takes Roy seventeen questions to uncover the reason. Lydia couldn't find a vacant conference room so she solved the problem by cancelling the meeting.

It's three-thirty before Roy gets a moment to look at the morning mail. Just as he eases into a long report, he's interrupted. In storms one of his section heads who seems completely unglued: "I've just got your margin comments on the M-4 startup and they are killing me. Six months ago you set this project in motion by asking a very specific set of questions. And, if you remember, *I* was the one who was concerned that your focus might be somewhat narrow. So we go out and do what you requested and eighteen man-months later you tell us that our report suffers from tunnel vision. My analysts look dumb for merely trying to be responsive to your structure. Frankly, Roy, I don't want to be around when they see your comments. You tell me what to say, but, by God, I'm going to say it came from you!"

Roy hears him out and to buy himself time he says, "I have an urgent call to return. Can you get back to me in 20 minutes?" Alone again, he considers how to respond.

Back again with the section head, it takes Roy two hours to get the monkey off his back and onto his section-head's where he almost feels it belongs. Roy refreshes the section head's memory, taking literary license as he goes, "You and I together made the decision to *appear* narrow on the front end but not actually to go narrow. We knew that's how we had to appear to get the startup okayed by Division management and we were in agreement that we were going to take some risks. It's risky all right, but if we survive the gains are going to be tremendous." Roy then goes into the technical details and the innovative reputation they can earn for their department. Roy acknowledges that the fight has just begun and asserts his commitment to going the extra rounds.

Eventually, Roy extracts agreement that this is the way to go and that the section head will support him and calm dissension within the ranks. At the conclusion Roy feels good about where he and the section head just came out but in pain from the day. Wearily he reaches for his coat and starts home. The section head feels mixed. He's disoriented and needs to replay the facts and the afternoon's portrayal of them. It's now his turn to retreat to his office to ponder his next move.

———————◆———————

Roy's day illustrates how self-interests are involved in every aspect of work and, from the standpoint of the organization, what a mixed bag they are. Self-interests energize people to go an extra round in the pursuit of excellence, such as Roy's risk-taking on the M-4 startup, but they can also be the basis for self-indulgence, such as the vice-president's coup in changing the manufacturing meeting to coincide with plans to attend a family gathering. However, differentiating between self-beneficial pursuits that cost the company and the ones from which it benefits is very difficult given the underground methods people use.

This story also illustrates why Roy had to operate the way he did. People weren't being straight with him and there was no way he was going to put a stop to it merely by acting honestly himself. His survival, his competence, and his sense of personal dignity always seemed to be on line. What could Roy tell his staff when he feared creating an irreparable breach of confidence, should they believe that his reasons for backing down to Cantrell were mainly political? What could he say to an R & D manager he hears mouthing a boy scout's notion of collaboration but disproving his words with his actions? How could he tell a key section head that the only way he knew to get a high-risk program like the M-4 startup moving was to deceive everybody in the line? And how could he respond to a longstanding friend who humiliated him by conceding that he's technically incompetent while thinking that he was doing Roy a big favor? Schisms were the only way to cope.

The way Roy operated is typical of how people in organizations push for what's personally important while holding off those who seem in the way. Roy thought "A" about his department's product-run analysis and said "Y". Cantrell thought "B" and said "Z". Then they held a conversation about Y and Z, each hoping to represent enough of A and B to take them to self-advantageous ground. Each colored meaning, shaded the truth, and presented biased accounts but tried never to tell an out-and-out lie. Getting caught would damage their credibility. Amazingly, we don't believe that Roy and Cantrell were all that conscious of what they were doing. We see them as we see most organization players, operating in knee-jerk fashion to create self-serving representations of the truth.

Are there costs associated with this way of operating? We think there are many. The most obvious involves a never ending cycle of corruption and deception, with each player viewing himself as merely a pawn in a game that is beyond his control. The result is that no one takes responsibility for the environment produced. No wonder Roy goes home in pain. With one exception, he went through a whole day without getting a straight story from anyone. The exception was Harry who wanted Roy to attest to the lie he told the production control manager.

Of course, Roy also dished it out. Each of his self-convenient versions of the truth switched the tables on someone else's picture of reality. Roy left a trail of disoriented subordinates, each wondering how he could be so myopic and feeling less than adequate about how he was doing his job. For example, Roy wound up questioning the assumptions on which the product-run analysis was based as if he would have preferred that his staff limit themselves to the going-in notions of corporate headquarters. And of course, there was the section head who, after two hours talking with Roy about the M-4 startup, went back to his office talking to himself.

———◆———

Eventually our search for an alternative to scenarios such as Roy's took us to the literature on organizations. We were looking for a way of managing self-interests that did not create additional subterfuge and conflict. Unfortunately, we were disappointed. We found a literature that fell into one of three mutually exclusive camps, each of which seems to promote the undisciplined expression of self-interests and subjectivity.

*First*, there is the *rational* view which considers self-interests to be the darker and undisciplined side of human nature and proposes the logic of objectivity for containing them. But everyone possesses the skills to marshall objective arguments in the service of pursuing vested interests, and the presence of this viewpoint makes it easy for people to do so.

*Next*, there is the *humanistic* view which assumes that by leveling with one another about what they've got personally and self-beneficially at stake, people will find ways to collaborate and work toward the greater good of the organization. But wherever we find people being direct and above board in stating their personal involvements, we find others using this openness to discredit their projects in the service of pushing their own self-beneficial pursuits.

*Finally*, there are the *personal power* theories which describe techniques the smart can use to gain more power and control at the other guy's expense. While these often work (certainly they are practiced in overabundance today), we abhor them because they subordinate the needs of the overall system and seem to escalate the conflict by furthering the self-beneficial interests of those who are most duplicitous.

———————

Our frustration with the literature provided us another insight into why people rely on schisms to get them through their organization day. Of course people keep their subjective interests hidden, they lack theories that tell them how to operate differently: In one way or another, everyone understands the omnipresence of self-interests, but people lack legitimate avenues either for expressing them or for helping others to channel them constructively. The undeniable need for an alternative way of operating, a theory to help people measure their self-interests against organizational priorities, has added energy to our search.

It has taken many years of thought, inquiry and experimentation for us to come up with a perspective that we believe offers a practical alternative to how people operate today. Our perspective is based on realizations that self-interests are the core of what brings meaning to a person's life at work; that all people possess the skills and inclination to pursue the self-beneficial in every aspect of their job, notwithstanding that some people are better at this than others; and that driving self-interests underground creates the condition for self-indulgence to flourish. What we have to propose is much more than just another openness theory. It's a way of thinking and operating that makes the personal components in one's participation more visible and makes individual variances from the organization's mission more apparent and available for discussion.

# THE SUBJECTIVE SIDE OF OBJECTIVE MANAGEMENT

II

Part I used the stories of Assemblyman Keysor and Roy to depict the four major themes of this book: (1) that self-interests play a decisive role in shaping every organizational event; (2) that people are at their peril when they openly reveal the self-interests that underlie their motivations; (3) that in not being able to acknowledge self-interests people have little choice but to engage in deceptive behavior which proves punishing to others and inefficient for the organization; and, (4) that we have a unique perspective on this state of affairs which should allow you to cope better, punish others less, and work for a change in the system.

Now that we've introduced you to our objectives we'd like to be more precise in showing you the subjective side of objective management. That's what the following four chapters are about.

Chapter 2 establishes what we see as the specific links between an individual's self-interests and what that person offers as "objective" statements of organizational mission, and the roles he or she thinks ought to be played. It depicts the arbitrary aspects of an individual's formula for success and the destructive competition that erupts between people with similar organizational goals but different talents and personal needs.

Chapter 3 examines the rational statements of commitment and responsibility that are asserted and debated as managers attempt to check self-interests and insure individual accountability. It shows how common sense approaches to accountability produce the illusion that self-interests are under control while transforming the fight to new and more covert ground.

Chapter 4 describes how self-interest battles are won and lost. It portrays the importance of keeping your adversaries on soil that is familiar to you and the self-interests involved in the rulings of those who present themselves as impartial referees and judges.

Chapter 5 concludes this section by presenting our scheme for seeing the roles self-interests play in determining how a person does his or her job and how that person sees and interprets subsequent organization events. Here we develop a perspective that should allow you to discriminate between self-interests which come at the expense of the organization and those which give the organization what it needs.

# 2 | IMAGE MANAGEMENT

We have found that succeeding in an organization is like trying to score at pocket billiards. The smart players always have two objectives. One is to put the ball in the pocket, and the other is to leave the cue ball in a position to successively put more balls in the pocket.

In other words, accomplishment is a necessary but insufficient step in staking out a strong organizational position. People must also use each action to put themselves in a better position to perform the next. And in order to do this, they must establish a set of images that cause their contributions first, to be recognized, and second, to be valued. That is, each person's success depends on getting others to see and appreciate the function his or her contribution performs for the organization. Only the naive assume that others will automatically recognize their contributions. The savvy appreciate that others have their own interests to push and may be in competition with them. To explain how competing self-interests create the need for self-beneficial organizational images, why establishing these images often entails warfare within the corporation, and why some images are notably more effective than others, we'll turn to an illustration.

———◆———

Charlie, the old pro, is about to transfer stateside. Having left the home office to develop the territory in Japan, it's time for another challenge. This means turning the Japanese business over to Marv, a manager whose ambitions and solid record of accomplishment make him a natural replacement.

Six years before this Charlie left the United States to start up the Japanese business from scratch. Through trial and error he had learned how to adjust United States practices to the most foreign of cultures. Not the least of his initial problems was gaining credibility from others in the corporation. Among other things, he had to convince them that his profit margins, which were low by United States standards, were as good as could be expected in Japan. He did such an outstanding job that now he's no longer harassed with questions about his "low" performance. In fact, his business is seen as healthy and he's seen as the cause of its success. Of course he wants these images to continue.

Consciously, Charlie wants what's best for the company and is anxious to pass on his hard learned lessons to his successor, Marv. Charlie knows he has deviated greatly from the United States model and wants to give Marv an appreciation of what's been accomplished and what needs to be done. What he doesn't realize is how much he needs Marv to endorse his logic.

Marv has also been around. He's valued, well-paid, but feels he hasn't received the corporate rank he deserves. The new assignment in Japan, however, affords him a real opportunity to change this situation. Since no corporate vice-president worth his perks passes up a chance to fly to Japan, Marv will be the host for a constant stream of brass. He'll have high visibility and plenty of opportunities to make his viewpoints known.

Consciously, Marv is a collaborator and wants to capitalize on Charlie's experience. But at some level he also understands that there's little to be gained by being known as the man who ran what Charlie created. No matter how healthy the business, his image depends on it looking different—and fast. His instincts tell him that his success depends on appearing to have solutions to the problems Charlie wasn't smart enough to spot. But this can't be talked about, even though it will become the first shell fired in what for him is to become a full-scale organizational war.

As an accommodation to Marv, Charlie agrees to fly to the United States to conduct a series of turnover briefings. Marv is busy getting his family and business affairs in order and needs this favor. Charlie begins their discussion with a description of the nuances and details necessary to appreciate the masterminding he's done. Although Marv makes every effort to signal gratitude for the care Charlie is taking, he has a difficult time concealing his impatience. Marv wants the big picture, the overview, but all he seems to get are the pieces. Normally Charlie is an expansive thinker and his meticulous sharing comes as an unpleasant surprise. Marv finds that efforts to quicken the pace only bog matters down more, since they send Charlie off explaining why hearing the details is important to understanding the reasons underlying what he did.

Adding to the awkwardness is Marv's keen interest in Charlie's unsolved problems and mistakes. Of course, from Marv's perspective this is where the opportunities lie. But his interest and questions put Charlie on the defensive. Charlie starts reacting badly, and when his irritation becomes too blatant he excuses himself on grounds that he's over-tired and a victim of jet lag.

Charlie is under tremendous pressure. The harder he works to get his concepts across, the more Marv seems to dismiss what he's saying. What's more, Charlie knows he mustn't sound overly possessive. To be seen this way should signal a lack of objectivity and give Marv the right to reject his perspectives out of hand.

---

Like most people who get involved in a fight like this, neither Marv nor Charlie recognizes how much a prisoner of the situation he is. Each takes the conflict personally, not realizing it's the way their situation is structured that pits them in battle against one another. Their fighting results from their need to create the images that allow them to succeed—but their prospects for finding a mutually compatible story are undercut by their inability to comprehend what they are facing.

An "outside" perspective reveals that the same situation presents Charlie and Marv with different challenges, and it's these differences that cause them to see and interpret things in competitive ways.

Marv's challenge is the most apparent. He knows he can't afford to be seen as a carbon copy of Charlie. What his gut understands, but his head doesn't quite, is that his eventual success rests on establishing a new set of images. He needs a new story for Japan—one that will give him room to succeed.

Charlie, who is already labeled a success, faces a less apparent challenge. However, in being less apparent, his is more like the ones most people face on a daily basis. He needs to protect a set of images about the function he performed and the general manager's role in its accomplishment—otherwise his activities won't be fully appreciated. Charlie doesn't understand the personal threat, nor his need to fight; all he has in mind is the health of the business and what's objectively needed to maintain it. Nevertheless, his reasons are more self-serving than his arguments divulge. In fact, the way he has things structured puts him in a death-struggle with Marv. There is no room for Marv to collaborate other than to pick up where Charlie left off.

———————————

We analyzed the situation and found that to be a success Charlie and Marv each needed to establish credible images in three domains of participation which we call mission, role and daily activities.

> *First*, their success depends on others seeing that the *mission* they address is essential to the health and productivity of the organization.

> *Second*, others must see the specific *role* they define for themselves as a credible and effective way of contributing to that mission.

> *Third*, others must see the link between the *activities* they engage in on a daily basis and the accomplishment of their specific role and organization mission.

Take away any of these three elements of credibility and they are dead. What's more, each must be on guard not to allow any one of these elements to become disconnected from the other two. That is, there is no success or credibility in being proficient in performing a role that is seen as irrelevant to the organization's purpose or in having daily activities seen as unrelated to the role and responsibilities others think should be assumed.

---

Almost from the start Charlie worked hard to promote the image that business in Japan is an entirely different ballgame and that its success rested on the company learning how to go "native." This became the unique *mission* he set about accomplishing. His fate hinged on whether the corporation would view his unit as one of Japan's top producers or one of the United States company's weakest profit centers. Thus Charlie worked hard to establish that deviation from the parent company's way of doing things and the development of new performance benchmarks were essential to measuring the success of his business.

This took some doing. Not only did he have to convince higher-ups but, hardest of all, he had to convince his own line managers. Each of them had technical bosses in the states who used performance measures at odds with what Charlie was trying to accomplish. His line managers' periodic disorientation, and their focus on the wrong standard, posed a constant threat to Charlie's story.

Once the Japan business was seen as different, Charlie had to define for himself a leadership role that meshed with the unique mission he had sold for the Japanese operation. Overall he promoted the image of enlightened leader and cultural broker. He emphasized that his was the role of attaining the proper mix of United States knowhow and the Japanese way. As he defined it, his role entailed recruiting top-notch United States personnel who could adopt the Japanese way, hiring Japanese nationals who could learn United States business practices and technologies, and interpreting his overall operation to stateside corporate management.

Lastly, Charlie's credibility rested on his ability to provide others with a roadmap for appreciating the unique way his daily activities fed the role he was attempting to perform and the mission he had set forth for the business. For Charlie, and for most senior-level managers, this was very difficult to do because on a daily basis high-level managers seldom accomplish anything tangible, they merely make a little progress toward a set of open-ended objectives. Because Charlie's job was so complex and his goals required working through people, his direct participation in organizational affairs was often a matter of nuance and difficult to perceive.

Charlie operated quite differently from the on-the-scene, autocratically inclined leader that characterized his company's management. His cultural broker role took him out of the office a great deal. He spent substantial amounts of time comparing notes with Japan-based executives of other United States companies and traveling to the United States on missions to brief bosses and candidates for jobs in his organization. Within the Japan office he used a derivative of consensus decision-making, à la Japan, and leader-led group problem-solving, à la United States. For example, he would bring his department heads together regularly to critique his business formulations and to discuss how their individual operations were doing. And he understood that unless he told his United States bosses why he was operating this way, they would lack the means for valuing what he was doing and would view his leadership as weak.

———————◆———————

Unfortunately for Charlie, Marv decided to score by declaring a new mission. Throughout the corporation he made it known that, "It's now time to turn the Japanese operation around and get it up to speed with the rest of the corporation" —a formulation that played right into the hands of the standard corporate mentality. He let everyone know that higher profit margins could be attained and that opening up the Orient was no different than opening up the Newark office. His declarations sent his department heads scurrying for cover. They began explaining their deviations from the United States way to orders from Charlie. Marv's angle on the business raised immediate questions about the essential tasks he found undone, each of which questioned the validity of what Charlie had been doing.

Marv chose the role of profit-booster, in a distinct contrast to the role Charlie had chosen for himself. As a result his daily activities focused on straightening out lines of authority and exercising control. Marv rode herd on managers who, he said, "had developed bad habits under a lax boss." He kept long hours, seldom stayed away from the plant for more than a day at a time, and instituted a new system of managerial controls that routed all financial matters to his desk for review before a final decision. He personally met with each manager to establish new and tighter budgets and generally acted as if the roof would come down on anyone whose department could not meet the profitability benchmarks practiced in the rest of the corporation.

———◆———

There are several lessons to this story.

*First*, it shows how success entails more than the objective outcomes of a specific assignment. It requires credibility in three domains of participation—mission, role and daily activities. To be sure, high quality performance and personal competence are important, but they are not sufficient to win organizational acclaim. Both Charlie and Marv are exceedingly competent and each did an outstanding job at what he set out to do. But had Marv not successfully gotten the definition of mission and role changed, his attention to profitability would have looked as irrelevant as Charlie's attention to cultural brokering eventually looked when reviewed against Marv's framework of profitability.

*Second,* this story illustrates how the artillery of organizational battles are meanings assigned to organizational events. Charlie's status hinged on whether Marv chose to position himself as a correction of the ills of Charlie's regime or of doing what was needed to respond to the next phase of the Japan business' development. Unfortunately, he chose a set of images that damaged Charlie, but he might have chosen a set portraying Charlie as a pioneer who did what was right at a point in time.

*Next,* this story shows how daily survival, let alone success, rests on never turning your back on someone who is in a situation where he or she has to fight, no matter how inadvertent and low-keyed the struggle may appear, and in developing a kind of street savvy for spotting meanings that pose a threat to your credibility. Marv actually believes he likes Charlie and intends him no harm. But his desire to do no more than what the rest of us are trying to do—succeed—has placed a smoking revolver in his hand. He did not know how to proceed without doing Charlie in, and Charlie did not know how to read the danger signs, thus presenting himself as an undefended target.

*Next,* this story depicts the subjective side of most evaluations. All evaluators have an image to push, and their reception of someone else's image is affected by how well their interests are served by it. Marv had no trouble switching the Japan mission on Charlie, making out as if Japan could tolerate the same business plan as Newark. After all, the company's executives understood Newark, and the idea that the United States framework could apply to Japan played into their needs to feel powerful. Some executives still believe that Japan requires its own way, but it will take years for them to reemerge with this view. We guess the school of hard knocks taught them the importance of staying out of the path of an organizational image that has momentum.

*Finally,* this story demonstrates the equifinality of organizational action. That is, there are infinite ways to pursue a specific role, endless definitions of role that can further a valued mission and even a number of definitions of mission that can earn the organization success—albeit, the pursuit of each definition will advance the organization at various rates on different performance criteria. The Japanese business will make more money with Marv, at least in the short run, but it had better personnel relations under Charlie, as well as a much better image in the Japanese business community. What's more, it will probably do something else under Marv's successor. In fact, the business can go "bad" and Marv's successor can make out all right by successfully selling a story about how much worse things would have gotten if someone hadn't stepped in and performed an essential mission in a particular way—a result of how badly Marv botched things by going all out in his push for profitability.

# 3 | ACCOUNTABILITY—THE FIGHT OVER COMMITMENT AND RESPONSIBILITY

The preceding chapter's story of Charlie and Marv illustrates the direct connection between an individual's desire for success and that person's skills in constructing an organizational reality that allows his or her accomplishments to be seen and valued. It also shows how the need for organizational images that support what one is uniquely about can bring people into life-and-death struggles with one another. But this story merely focuses on two players and a single outcome.

From a slightly broader perspective, it becomes obvious that Charlie and Marv aren't the only ones who must establish organizational images that allow them to succeed. Most of the people with whom they work will also be striving to create self-convenient images of their own. And by necessity the self-interests on which these images are based will be hidden and argued within the guise of advocating what's good for the organization. This brings us to the big question.

*Given that everyone has the skills to run his or her own pattern while calling it organization effectiveness, how do managers control against excesses in the expression of self-interests and get others to agree on their respective roles in accomplishing the organizational tasks at hand?*

———————◆———————

Actually most managers are able to get "product" out the door and succeed in getting their organizations to turn a good profit. And we find that those who do the best are those who put a great deal of effort into controlling against excesses in other people's pursuit of self-interests. They do this by trying to specify the types of commitment and responsibility needed to make their organizations go. They present what needs to be done and how it should be accomplished with the idea that eventually an agreement will be struck and that everyone will stand accountable for his or her role in producing what's been agreed upon.

However, most managers appreciate that it's far easier to strike an agreement than to enforce one. Thus to ensure accountability and pin others down they reach for concrete standards. Some emphasize responsibility, either by specifying the inputs (the actions or levels of effort others are expected to contribute) or by specifying the outputs (the results or tangible accomplishments others are expected to produce). Some emphasize commitments by specifying the quality and intensity of impact and involvement others are expected to sustain. And some emphasize combinations of the above. Specifying inputs, outputs, and/or impacts allows a manager to scrutinize someone's efforts by raising such fundamental questions as:

INPUTS — *Did you make the required effort and did you follow the rules, procedures, and special instructions?*

OUTPUTS — *Did you produce the agreed-upon bottom-line product?*

IMPACTS — *Did your efforts and accomplishments have an overall favorable effect on the wider world and leave the productive capacity of the system intact?*

On the face of it these seem like perfectly reasonable questions or standards to invoke in protecting against excesses in the expression of self-interests and ensuring committed and responsible organizational participation. Unfortunately, these standards sound much better in theory than they work in practice. Although they do squeeze out gross self-indulgence and establish concrete performance expectations, they do not eliminate the pursuit of basic self-interests of the type we've been discussing in this book. People put just as much effort as they ever did into trying to establish definitions of task and role that make it possible for them to succeed. Their ideas of organizational effectiveness and personal potency depend on this.

Thus each *absolute* promise to deliver inputs, produce results, and have an impact on the system is a matter of *relatives* and can only be understood in the context of the unique characteristics of those involved. Self-interests, finite energies, and the need to succeed with imperfect skills will always influence how an assignment gets construed. And because these factors cannot be discussed directly, what seems to be a simple straightforward approach to ensure accountability quickly becomes a major managerial challenge.

In their zeal to meet this challenge and extract accountable performances, managers resort to treating their input, output, and impact proposals as absolutes that are supposed to hold regardless of what's personally at stake for those involved and regardless of how the situation actually unfolds. That which is unique to the manager's view of the world, and consistent with that person's needs to have the job defined in a way that allows him or her to succeed, is portrayed as an organizational imperative with the implication that those who fail to produce as specified are either inept, self-indulgent, or disloyal.

However, such attempts to overpower basic self-interests often lead to serious distortions in organizational purpose. Absolute statements of input, output, and impact put people in binds where, in order to pursue what is personally important, they comply with all the stipulated procedures and fail to produce bottom-line results; where they produce bottom-line results and neglect the well-being of the wider systems; and where they make lofty commitments to impact the system and fail to achieve the tangible accomplishments which real impact requires. To show how managers self-conveniently set absolute standards and how the way people respond can distort organization purpose, we turn to a series of illustrations.

---

### Inputs

Inputs are the first standards managers reach for when trying to enforce accountability. Dissatisfied evaluators point to the "absolutely" essential operations that were not performed and the procedures that were not observed which they contend are the ingredients of any satisfactory performance. They cite organizational givens as if they would similarly fault anyone who missed touching all the bases regardless of the results produced. It's the self-convenient logic a division manager resorts to when called on to explain why he wants to fire his marketing manager, despite the fact that this manager has met the bottom-line objectives of building up division sales. He attempts to present a convincing case by referring to a lax attitude, an unspent advertising budget, and a messy office as if these factors conclusively demonstrate a marginal performance.

Conversely, performers point to their inputs, to the fact that they followed all the established procedures and made quality contributions in a timely fashion, when faced with a critical evaluation of a project's results. It's the rationale the engineer falls back on when put on the carpet because the bridge he designed collapses. He points out how he performed all operations specified, thus claiming the disaster wasn't his fault.

Attempting to gain accountability through the use of absolute definitions of inputs is a logical approach to checking self-interests in an organizational world in which such interests cannot openly be discussed. However, it is a costly approach particularly when employed by high-level managers such as the executive committee of a major computer manufacturer. It got them into considerable trouble when they used it to deal with the problems created when their star salesman's commissions approached the annual salary of the corporation's president. They might have raised the president's pay, but instead they decided to place a $275,000 ceiling on salesman earnings. We would characterize this response as "absolute," because it focused on salary equity devoid of consideration for salesman and company performance. How did the star salesman respond to their action? He worked harder than ever, made his ceiling in the first quarter, and spent the rest of the year formulating plans to set up a competing company which, three years later, significantly cut into the profits of the siring corporation.

### Outputs

Justifying one's actions on grounds of inputs infuriates evaluators whose needs aren't being served by that which is being produced. In response they take the accountability battle to the place where they think it belongs, hard results. "Let's examine output," they say, "that's the bottom line, isn't it?"

On the face of it, outputs are easy places to institute real accountability. Agree on objectives and hold people accountable for achieving them. If they don't, bring in the next crew. Right? Wrong. It's just not that easy because one can easily produce results without achieving his or her organizational purpose.

For example, people who follow professional football readily agree that the punter lives a highly visible existence and that the record of his performance, average yards per kick, is as revealing a statistic as any player faces in having his results measured. Well, several years ago we watched Atlanta's league-leading punter in action at a Los Angeles Rams–Atlanta Falcons game. Playing for a weak team, he entered the game with a 46-plus yards per kick punting average. Now test your skills for discerning responsible performance: how do you account for the fact that following a booming 75-yard kick the punter was verbally abused by his coach and teammates, and after the game relegated to a backup role, never, to our knowledge, to return as a primary punter for any other team in the league?

———◆———

Here was the situation.

The game was scoreless, time was running out, and both teams' defenses looked solid. It seemed like a day when breaks and field position would determine the outcome. The Falcons had the ball on the 48 yard line of what had been billed to be a much stronger Ram team. It was a perfect opportunity for the Falcon's punter to hang one up in the wind, or go for the corner, in order to pin the Rams deep in their own territory. But instead he kicked the hell out of the ball. In fact, the ball sailed clear out of the end zone. The length of the kick made it obvious that he didn't just muff it. So the punter got credit for a 48-yard kick from scrimmage, which strengthened his average, but the ball automatically came back to the Rams' 20, a net of only 28 yards for the Falcons.

Analyzing this situation, we can begin to see the confusion which surrounds any absolute measure of output. From the coach's viewpoint it was a clear-cut case of the punter viewing his outputs as distinct from the team results; what else could account for his insensitivity to the team situation and his decision to go for average? However, the next morning's paper revealed the punter's side of the story. It seems that last winter when the terms of this year's contract were negotiated, the coach resisted the punter's request for a pay increase because of his low yards-per-kick average the year before. In this context, a demonstrated ability to kick the ball over 46 yards per try constituted a bona fide concept of output responsibility and good reason to justify a pay hike.

Thus we see that outputs, their type and value, cannot be assessed independently from the impact the people exercising and experiencing them are trying to achieve and that each performance can only be understood in terms of the realities of the actual participants. Unlike popular conception, there is nothing absolute about responsibility—what constitutes satisfactory inputs and what is the desired output. Come contract time, the coach is likely to again shift his argument 180 degrees when it is to his advantage to use a low punting average as synonymous with poor output effectiveness and a punter would have to work like the dickens to reconstruct all the occasions in which he sacrificed average for the good of the team.

---

### Impact

Impact is the final standard people use in trying to ensure accountability. They do so out of the realization that it is possible to produce desired outcomes that fail to accomplish the ultimate mission. Evaluators say, "Let's agree in advance about what you stand for and then let's assess your results." Sounds straightforward, doesn't it? Look again.

Finding out in advance what an individual stands for is an appealing thought. It seems to offer evaluators one last chance to sleep nights, knowing that desired outcomes will not be disconnected from the over-arching impact they were intended to produce. Evaluators want to hear that one is orienting to higher-order institutional objectives and that all the efforts that will be marshalled in the service of meeting those objectives are as yet unspecified. That is, evaluators want to know that one stands "open-endedly" ready to do whatever is called for as specific situations evolve. The television sponsor wants to know that his show's producer will not content himself with high Nielson ratings and forget good taste. The plant manager wants to know that in setting production records his manufacturing manager is neither going to burn up the equipment nor neglect standards of quality. And concerned parents want to know that their child's high scores in reading are not coming at the expense of a good social adjustment.

Unfortunately, even when it comes to impact, evaluators reach for absolutes. Usually they have their own ideas about what's needed for institutional effectiveness and make it known that they're ready to do battle over the differences. They seek to create organizational imperatives with little, if any, respect for the vested interests that underlie a conflicting position. And if you think inputs and outputs stimulate tough accountability fights, you ought to see the ones provoked by different open-ended commitments to impact. Not only are factors which are relative called "absolutes," but people get quite moralistic. For instance, consider what the director of mental health services for Los Angeles County faces as he tries to pursue an open-ended commitment to mental illness *prevention* in a system that appears only capable of supporting treatment for those who are already ill.

The director's commitment to prevention pits him in an uphill battle for funds. He faces a fiscal situation made conservative by spiraling inflation and a governor who, early in his administration, made it known that he would view all the "rehabilitative" programs (drugs, alcohol, mental health, etc.) with a skeptical eye. The governor indicated that those programs would receive a minimal amount of good faith funding, but would have to demonstrate their ultimate rehabilitative impact before even their existing budgets would be renewed. And since 90 cents of every mental health dollar spent by Los Angeles County comes from the state, the director must pay a good deal of attention to what the governor wants.

The director hears the governor asking him to justify mental health expenditures on the narrowest possible dimension—one that lacks relevance to the major opportunity he sees before him. The governor's willingness to fund mental health rests on what he calls the hard results—the number of hospitalized patients returned to the community. But this measure neglects the work done in keeping people out of hospitals. It means spending the bulk of the county's funds on people who have retreated either close to or beyond the point where they can be reached with professional help. In contrast, the director wants to find small centers in the community which focus on intervention at the incipient stages of illness and on educational programs aimed at derailing the social conditions that produce mental stress. His open-ended commitment leads him to a concept of reaching towards mental health rather than to attacking mental illness.

---

Fights between people with commitments to different impacts can usually be tied to the scope of each person's job concerns, an area where self-interests are deeply involved. Consistent with his concerns the governor essentially says,

"Without the statistics that force me to readjust my priorities, I'm hard pressed to deliver any increase in funds and if other state units, like the department of highways, can justify why they need more, then I'm going to give you less." In response the director struggles to assert his commitment by saying something like, "You've got a narrow view of mental health and you've got to give me more support or I'll falter in monitoring what's actually taking place in the community and in positioning us to capitalize on the real opportunities for impact."

Fights over commitments to impact take place at three levels.

*The first level* finds each of the adversaries claiming that the other is "closed-ended" in an important area where he or she is "open-ended"—ready to do whatever is required to get the job done—and hence more virtuous. Differences in commitment cause both the governor and the director to claim that the other is being unresponsive to the people he is mandated to serve. The director claims the governor's brand of hard results leaves no other options than to pour money into high cost, low payoff, mental asylums. Conversely, the governor claims that the director is lost in the problems of Los Angeles County, willing to take funds at the expense of anyone from the department of highways to mental health in San Francisco County.

*The second level* finds the adversaries disparaging the other's commitments and substituting their own. The governor asserts something like, "Hey look, I'm as committed as you to helping the unfortunate but the reality is that this is a period of limited resources. Sometimes I get the feeling that your notion of commitment begins and ends with lobbying my office for extra money. I'm already funding you to the tune of $150 million a year! Why don't you use that to achieve a better balance between the community care you prize so much and getting people out of hospitals and into the real world where they belong? Come on, act more responsible! This is an era of limits, and everyone has to give."

In response the director attempts a disparaging response that runs like, "Your budget cutbacks have already squeezed us to the point where all of our resources are needed to attend to the needs of the acute and chronically ill. Your policies put us in a vicious cycle. Without a preventative program there is going to be an increasing population of chronically ill requiring extended periods of high-cost institutional care. Ten years from now we'll find ourselves spending twice what we are now, accomplishing little more than keeping the acutely disturbed off the streets."

*The third level* in the fight over commitments usually finds one of the adversaries going for the proverbial throat. This is done by feigning consideration of the other person's open-ended commitments and then challenging the other person on his or her ability to deliver tangible results. In this case it was the governor who became the most aggressive. We interpreted him as saying, "Even if I shared your dream, I'd have to challenge you on whether such a concept can work in practice. For twenty years mental health advocates have been parading this vision before us and I have yet to learn of any preventative program which has significantly cut the numbers of people being hospitalized with acute mental illness. What's more, even if such a preventative program were feasible, I have real doubts as to whether Los Angeles County is the place where it could be successfully implemented. After all, your people barely seem able to manage the programs you already have."

The governor's arguments leave the director few places to go. He can't allow his operation to be judged on the terms set down by the governor—the rehabilitation of deeply disturbed patients. Doing so sets him up to be evaluated at his weakest point of impact, for few cures exist for patients who are disturbed enough to be hospitalized. On the other hand, attempting to hold out and sell a broader concept of mental health, such as the one contained in the community mental health center model, means incurring the criticisms that come from requesting extra funds at a time when cutbacks are the order of the day.

Neither of these alternatives could be worse than the tack seized on instinctively by any number of mental health administrators pursuing open-ended commitments similar to the one held by our director. Their instinct, in the face of tight funding, has been to fight on fraudulent grounds. They reason that the virtues of their open-ended commitment justify all-out war. They have sought to arouse public support by painting pictures of homicidal maniacs stalking the streets and dead bodies buried in the backyards of mental hospitals. Such stories produce funds all right. It gets them the dollars they need but at the cost of reinforcing the very stigmas that keep people from seeking out professional help in the early-warning stages of mental crisis.

Unfortunately, people can never count on overlaps between their own vested interests and those of their evaluators. Instead, they are likely to find themselves being evaluated on criteria they never set out to meet. As a result, the evaluators may label their best efforts as inadequate, or portray their commitments as totally traceable to personal and self-beneficial stakes. In fits of pique the director links the governor's "tough-minded" stand on mental health to the governor's ambitions for higher office. Likewise, we can conjecture that at moments of high frustration the governor sees the director as a careerist, out to expand his operation without concern for the public's benefit.

Actually, commitments are matters of gradations, and if we were being precise we'd be talking about the degree of open-endedness in an individual's commitment. Even the director is closed to some alternatives that might prove more beneficial than the community-centered model he favors and, as the governor implies, he doesn't seem to give a hoot about mental health in San Francisco County. Similarly, each person has finite energies and biases that are determined by that person's interests and skills. There are degrees to which people are open to alternatives, even when they vow to go all out.

———————◆———————

This chapter illustrates how fights over self-interests—over whose definitions of mission and role and ideas of the activities needed to support those definitions will prevail—are transposed to what organizational participants would have us believe are rational disagreements over which definitions of impact, output, and input best move the organization ahead. Notwithstanding the agreements some people come to as they hit upon mutually compatible statements of commitment and responsibility, it looks to us as if just as many self-interests get packaged in with the way each individual defines his or her commitments and discharges his or her responsibilities as people are trying to protect against in the first place. Incompatible self-interests remain incompatible, they just get played out in another form.

Thus, in the conduct of daily organizational affairs, the statements of purpose and contribution which individuals portray as "absolutely" essential to the organization's effectiveness, and the efforts they claim demonstrate an adequate exercise of someone's responsibilities, usually reflect as much self-convenience as organizational contribution. Will the emphasis be on getting people out of psychiatric hospitals or preventing breakdown? Was the misguided punt an error of execution or of poor management? Is the idea to preserve a disciplined pay scale or to reward the best salesman the computer industry has ever seen? What gets portrayed as essential turns out to be a matter of relatives with efforts to control against excessive expressions of self-interests and to create accountability to the external organization often becoming more illusionary than real.

# 4 | WINNING AND THE FIGHT OVER ORIENTATION

We've just seen how people who hold very different perspectives on what is needed to make an organization effective are each able to formulate credible arguments to justify their beliefs and how self-interests lie beneath all that they advocate. Self-interests determine how an individual portrays what's needed externally as well as the commitments and responsibilities that person follows internally. Now the question is:

*What determines whose self-convenient definitions, or orientation, wins out and whose internal perspective prevails?*

Our answer begins with an illustration intended to take you inside a typical conflict over self-interests and to show you how to predict whose orientation will prevail. There is a surprise here, for unlike most fights, the victor cannot be predicted on the basis of which side draws the most blood or has the superior position to defend. Instead, it's the ground on which the fight gets fought and the orientation that best fits with the self-interests of those viewing the fight that decides who wins. The key to victory lies in keeping the opposition debating within a structure that supports your position while appealing to the interests of your viewers, and switching tracks once an opponent starts to score. The successful advocate switches between attacking his or her adversary's commitments to impact, output, and input, in order to keep the discussion on a compatible track. In fact, maintaining the discussion within a compatible structure turns out to be even more important than the specific points which are scored. Follow along with us and see whether you can spot these switching tactics and predict the victor in a conflict that took place in the driveway of a large condominium complex down the street from where we go to write.

---

Bert, an officer of the complex's governing board, takes to task Herb, a condominium owner, for washing his car in the midst of a severe California water shortage. Herb is infuriated—imagine anyone challenging his right to wash his car and calling him a "water-waster"!

BERT — Don't you know there's a water shortage and the board has ruled that our water is not meant for cars?

HERB — If I can't wash my car here, how do you expect me to get it washed?

BERT — Do like I do, take it to the car wash.

HERB — But the car wash uses fifty times as much water per car as the two buckets I'm using. Is that what the board means by saving water? What's your real problem?

BERT — My beef is dollars. I can't control what the car wash does, but I do know that if the complex doesn't reduce its water consumption by 20 percent we're going to get fined. Didn't you read in the paper last week where the university got fined $20,000. Are you going to pay the fine if we exceed our quota?

HERB — (Pointing to his two buckets) Since you asked, I'll be more than willing to pay the fine on the eight buckets a month I use. Let's see, at current rates that would total about 25 cents. (Herb then reaches in his pocket and pulls out a dollar and offers it to Bert.)

BERT — Look, let's not get technical, the board of governors has passed a rule forbidding the use of complex water for car washing and all I'm trying to do, as an officer of the board, is to enforce the rule in a fair and even-handed way. Now, are you going to stop washing your car or not?

HERB — I never saw the announcement in any of the material from the board regarding the water shortage. Are you sure the board passed such a rule?

BERT — What—are you calling me a liar? I've been an officer of the board for seven years. Do you think I've got nothing better to do than make up rules and run around singling out residents for punishment? Look, I don't have time to stand around jabber-jawing with anti-social assholes who refuse to take any responsibility for water conservation. I've tried to ask you nicely, but I guess for a troublemaker like you it's going to take a special censoring to get you to comply. (With that he storms away.)

This story was chosen because it illustrates in one brief but explosive encounter the inner workings of the fights people have over the way commitments and responsibilities get defined and exercised in their organization. Very quickly, let's re-run the debate to examine the underlying framework and score the arguments on a round-by-round basis.

Bert led with an appeal to his commitment—conservation of water. Stripped bare his message read, "Herb, refusing to stop washing your car makes you a bad citizen of California." Herb counterattacked by challenging the validity of Bert's appeal and substituting his own definition of water conservation. He said, "In light of the alternatives (handwash or minute carwash) the truly concerned citizen will choose the alternative that is best for the state, and not limit himself to what's best for the condominium." A major point for Herb.

Sensing Herb closing in, Bert switched from an argument based on his commitment to impact to one based on outcomes and responsibility. He essentially said, "If you continue to wash your car, our complex will be required to pay a penalty with the result that other members of this residential community will suffer financial loss due to your independent and unwarranted actions." Once again, Herb's rejoinder was designed to deflate the force of Bert's definition of responsibility. He said, "I accept full financial responsibility for the 'piddling' amount of water involved in the washing of my car," and offered him a dollar.

Another major point for Herb, time once again for Bert to switch tracks. This time he switched from an output definition of responsibility, the penalty for excessive water usage, to an input definition of responsibility (the rules and his authority). Bert essentially said, "By refusing to stop washing your car, you are failing to comply with the rules established by elected representatives for the overall good of complex residents."

Finally, Bert scores a point, albeit on a technicality. While Herb could self-righteously contend that he was committing neither an economic nor social misdemeanor, there was no way he could deny that he was not in violation of the rules passed by the board. In response Herb "played dumb," saying, "I refuse to accept the existence of such a rule until I see it in writing."

Who won the battle? Let's add it up. Two major points for Herb and one technicality for Bert. Looks like Herb is the victor, right? Wrong. Just listen to what was exchanged between Herb and his wife a few minutes later as he waltzed in savoring his apparent triumph. Point by point Herb explained how he demolished each of Bert's arguments and reduced him to a fist-shaking old man. In response she said, "What's the percentage in standing out there on a hot day beating up on an 85-year-old man?! After all, he was only trying to save water, protect the complex from a heavy fine, and carry out the wishes of a board *we* helped to elect." The winner? Bert by a knock out!

How do we explain the outcome?

*First*, battles over self-convenient definitions of commitment and responsibility, over whose orientation prevails, are not decided by the protagonists alone, they are also decided by the viewers.

*Second*, each viewer has his or her own ax to grind which determines the sentiments with which that viewer observes the action.

*Third*, whether or not viewers are able to seize a situation to push their own interests depends upon whose structure or framework the debate gets fought.

In this instance, it was clear that Herb's wife had her own agenda to push. Herb is equally self-righteous in his dealings with her and here was an opportunity to shape him up while wearing the guise of a neutral observer. Had the debate been carried out on Herb's turf, had Herb succeeded in getting Bert to come to his structure, say by debating the amounts of water consumed at the car wash or costs to the complex, his wife probably would have passed up this chance to choose sides. She would have sensed that getting on Herb's case would have shown her up as biased and discredited her argument. Then Herb would have been the victor, even in Bert's mind.

---

Likewise, in organizations, the structure or ground on which an issue is fought is a necessary, but not sufficient, condition for predicting who wins a battle over orientations. Establishing the ground is a major factor but it can be cancelled out by a viewer's vested interests. Does this mean that corruption is involved? We think not necessarily. Most viewers do not go out consciously trying to exploit a situation for personal gain. It's what they actually see that determines what they say. But they watch organization happenings the same way most of us watch a sporting event in which our home-town or school favorite is playing. The team we're backing either runs a good play or a poor one. *They* either win it or *they* blow it. In fact, the fine points and talents of the other team often don't register in our recount of the action. Similarly, organization viewers clock the action with the bias of home team rooters and don't observe all participants or their contributions with equal sensitivity and empathy.

Thus we can see the politics of daily life within an organization where contributing to the organization effort is one thing, but having your contributions valued entails packaging them so that others will want to see their value. Consider what we've concluded about the inner politics of organization life:

- Third parties almost always view organization happenings from the vantage point of how events personally affect them and their own orientations to the organization.

- Whether or not third parties choose to value what is contributed depends on how well they see that contribution supporting and complementing that which they are self-conveniently pursuing.

- Whether or not third parties decide to take a stand and publicly support or criticize a contribution or perspective, depends on whether they think this can be done in a way that leaves their credibility intact and keeps their vested interests hidden.

- Since no definition of organizational reality fits all, people bargain and negotiate in their interpretations of each event, trying to find an interpretation that best serves a critical mass of self-interests, including their own.

- The large number of plausible organization realities makes it possible to find a perspective that devalues just about any contribution, and the constant threat that this might occur keeps people insecure and on the alert for others who may be out to push a meaning that renders their reality ineffective.

- In being ever sensitive to the meanings others attach to events, people constantly angle to support others whose orientations are compatible with their own and to block those whose orientations come at the expense of valuing that which they are trying to contribute.

To make these points clearer, we'd like to present you with a scheme we've worked up for depicting the everyday politics involved in whether someone gets their contributions and job orientation valued.

Our scheme likens each person's effort to a vector whose direction is determined by that person's orientation and whose length represents excellence in the direction of that orientation. People with decidedly different personal pursuits will have vectors pointed in very different directions, people with comparable pursuits but different proficiencies will have vectors of varying lengths. For instance, the vector of person A can be represented as:

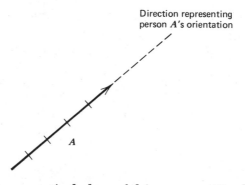

Vectors are particularly useful in representing how an individual's efforts are valued by others because their lengths depend on the orientation of the person viewing them. That is, a compatible orientation produces a "vector resolve," the perpendicular shadow cast on a line portraying the direction of the viewer's orientation, which is almost as long as person A's actual thrust—see $A_1$ below.

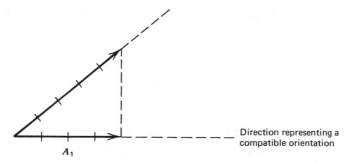

An incompatible orientation, one based on a set of commitments that vary a good deal from the ones which orient the contributor, produces a vector resolve that is nowhere near as long as the person A's actual thrust—see $A_2$ below.

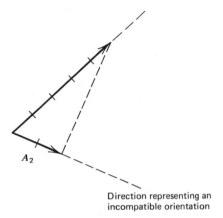

Direction representing an
incompatible orientation

In this way we could portray another car-washer overhearing the Herb and Bert debate as valuing Herb's performance with $A_1$ strength, while Herb's wife, with her axe to grind, reduced the length of Herb's vector to $A_2$.

Thus we have a schematic way of portraying how the value attached to one's outputs, and contributions, and the images of mission, role and daily activities one puts forth in developing credibility for them, depends on the orientation of one's viewers. It shows how the vested interests and political realities surrounding one's organizational contributions can create the conditions that bend and reduce the length of one's vector. And if there's anything that characterizes the effects of the war of meanings, it's the number of people running around organizations today with bent vectors!

# 5 | ALIGNMENT

Thus far we have sketched a web of inevitable subjectivity. We have identified how self-interests are concealed in the images people present, the roles they assume, the tasks they attempt, and the evaluations they make. We've even given you some guides to predicting the outcomes of the conflicts self-interests generate. But, just recognizing that self-interests are pervasive won't guarantee either that you can discern the particular interests an individual is trying to push, or understand how your own interests affect your perception of them. If, potentially, there are an infinite number of ways to specify a role, infinite definitions of mission that can earn the organization success, and infinite vantage points from which to evaluate these roles and missions, what determines the specific way an individual decides to perform a job or interpret a situation? Why do people with comparable organizational goals see the same situation differently and fight unyieldingly over which interpretation is correct, even when they are not competing for recognition? Why do people with the same job perform their assignments so differently?

———————◆———————

Our illustrations have suggested that our answer is in some way linked to organization politics and the self-interests connected with the individual's desire for success and recognition. Yet, at the same time our observations have shown that the diversity of interests that people weave into their jobs can not be explained on the basis of self-interests alone. Accordingly our answers to the questions we've posed and explanations of this variety rest on several important observations.

*First,* we find relatively few people who measure their success solely on the basis of external rewards: how far they've made it in the hierarchy, how much money they earn, and how much praise they receive. Most people claim that they're primarily concerned with internal satisfactions, such as finding opportunities to pursue personal interests and values, to learn and develop personally, and to demonstrate skills in areas of their special competence.

*Second,* we find that the unique definition of success each person holds, and the unique set of objectives toward which that person is targeted cannot be deduced merely by observing what he or she is doing.

*Third,* we find that knowing an individual's unique definition of success and his or her reasons for holding it allows us to see self-interests in how each assignment is performed, each problem is formulated and each organization event is viewed.

*Fourth,* we find that achieving a brand of success that is

internally meaningful, and not just aimed at gaining organizational acclaim, rests on an individual's ability to, at one moment, satisfy internal needs and meet what he or she sees as the objective needs of the job.

*And fifth,* we find that there are not enough minutes in the day to pursue self and organizational interests independently, nor do people possess the mental resources to keep self and organizational interests from intermingling.

Thus we find that success involves much more than scoring on the organization checklist. It entails both scoring and ensuring that the checklist doesn't preempt what is personally important. To accomplish this an individual must find a way to remain true to internal values but remaining true to internal values is no easy assignment. For instance, consider the problem a professor friend of ours uncovered as his wife observed the effects of a particularly harrowing day.

> She asked, "Well, did you at least accomplish something?" He answered, "Absolutely nothing, I wasted the entire day talking with students." She shot him one of those looks a knowing wife can deliver, and he thought a minute about what he said. "After all," he reflected, "I took an academic job because I enjoy teaching and counseling students and here I am complaining."

Until his wife caught him, our colleague was disoriented. He works in a system in which writing is the most important criterion for promotion, and in which publishing is equated with success. Because he was focusing on these priorities, he lacked a means for seeing accomplishment on a day when he wasn't making any headway on either of them. It took a signal from his wife and a reassertion of personal values to put him back in touch with an orientation that valued interactions with students.

Likewise, each of us needs a means of keeping in touch with

the inner themes that direct us while attending to the organization business at hand. We need a way of relating to situations and of structuring all that is important to us. Part of what is important is achieving excellence in organization projects, part is achieving accomplishment in one's career, and part is achieving personal meaning. Since each person has a unique set of interests and values to realize and a unique set of skills and competencies to display, each person's structuring of events will be as different as his or her thumbprint.

### Self-Interests and Organization Needs

Each time people enter a new work situation they engage in the implicit process of *aligning* personal values, interests, and skills with what they perceive to be the task requirements of their job. They seek an orientation that maximizes self-pursuits and organizational contribution. *Alignment* is our term for the orientation that results from such an effort, however implicitly this takes place. Once such an orientation has been evolved, it becomes a self-convenient lens through which all organizational happenings are viewed. That is, once people hit on an alignment—an orientation that lines self-interests up with the task-requirements of their jobs—this alignment serves to alert them to meanings they can use in promoting and supporting their personal and organizational endeavors, and to meanings put forth by others which threaten the credibility and relevance of what they are pursuing.

Not all alignments are effective. That is, the orientation some people use is too far removed either from the needs and obligations of their jobs or from expressing the inner themes that can make their job personally meaningful. We say an individual possesses an "effective" alignment when the orientation directing that person's actions and view of reality allows him or her to represent important self-interests while making a contribution to the organization. We say an individual lacks an effective alignment when important discrepancies exist between what that person inwardly values, endeavors to express, does well, and needs to do in order to satisfy what he or she perceives to be the task requirements of the job.

Now we can return to the questions raised at the beginning of this chapter.

> *Why do people with the same job perform their assignments so differently?*

Easy, they have unique interests, values, and competencies to bootleg into their jobs at every opportunity.

> *Why do people with comparable organizational goals see the same situation differently and fight unyieldingly over which interpretation is correct?*

Easy, while they may be striving to attain comparable organizational objectives, what they are striving to attain in their lives and careers is very different. This causes them to attend differently to each of the elements in a given situation. Finally,

> *What determines the specific way individuals decide to perform their jobs and how they interpret each situation?*

Easy again, it's what we've termed alignment. People proceed with a job orientation that spontaneously spins out interpretations and meanings that serve the unique way they need reality constructed in order to be a "success." How individuals do a job and what they see are influenced by what they find personally interesting, by the concepts they can master and the skills they can perform with excellence, by the self-ideals and values they seek to attain, by their unique ideas of what constitutes career advancement, by what they believe will score on the checklist that others will use in evaluating their performance, and by what they genuinely believe the organization needs from someone in their role.

———————◆———————

Few people are all that aware of their alignment. Even fewer are conscious of the fact that systematic biases permeate their view of the organizational world. And, almost no one understands that such biases play a major role in making organizations effective. All this is because most people work their alignment out implicitly and take its presence for granted until a change in the external scene, in other people's views of their effectiveness, or in their own sense of satisfaction show it to be obsolete. Then they can appreciate what they lost and strive for a new alignment that will again allow them to satisfy self-interests and personal pride while getting acclaim for doing a good job. For example, consider what happened to a middle manager named Pete who had a marvelous alignment until he got promoted and suddenly found himself faced with a serious gap between his own and the organization's definition of success.

Pete was one of twenty in his corporation who, some five years ago, agreed to take on a newly created mission, that of improving communications and managerial competence within his company. This function seemed right up Pete's alley. He'd attended sensitivity training sessions, had a reputation of being genuinely concerned with people, and was respected up and down the ranks for his leadership ability even though he had not burned up the track with his progress.

Pete saw the new assignment as a chance to bolster a lagging career. He had never been overly concerned with rising in the hierarchy, but his failure to take a fast track to the top was presenting him with daily redundancies that left him feeling somewhat stale. At forty-five he needed another challenge and this assignment held the potential to revitalize his career. Eagerly he accepted.

Pete threw himself into the new position. He enrolled in outside courses and hired skilled consultants to design training programs for the corporation's managers. Whenever possible he assisted the consultants and within a short time he understood their technology and was able to play a role in tailoring their inputs to the specific needs of his corporation. His learning continued and soon he was running programs on his own, involving personnel from each divisional level. Almost immediately his reputation as a man who genuinely cared was enhanced by widespread recognition of his competence in the management development technologies. And he was no soft touch either. He aggressively challenged managers on their "self-sealing" logics and constructed boat-rocking experiments to confront higher-ups with the demotivating and profit-eroding consequences of their autocratic styles.

Pete's involvements took an exciting turn with the advent of minority and women's consciousness. If the corporation's managers weren't racist, their de facto hiring and promotion policies were. This meant a greater volume of work and warranted an increase in the size of his staff. From a resource base that started with himself and a secretary, his department increased to two professionals, an administrative assistant, and two secretaries. Their operation hummed. They did career development counseling with secretaries. They got involved with the corporation's recruiters, both to encourage the hiring of blacks and females and to create programs that would support the new employees' progress in an essentially all white male management structure. They hired racial-awareness consultants to get managers in touch with their prejudices and help them work these out. And with this heightened workload,

Pete even found time to continue his efforts in getting managers to identify areas in which their style intruded on the effectiveness of others.

Pete also had marvelous latitude in job definition which he exploited to match his interests and values. He enrolled in personal growth courses, attended conventions, joined professional associations, and on occasion even used the company plane. Because Pete identified both with the welfare of people and the productivity of the corporation and was concerned that his work produce tangible outcomes, his indulgences were hardly noticed—rather they were seen as part of his power. The people on his staff looked up to him and nondefensively brought him their toughest problems for coaching and support. His credibility with people lower in the hierarchy provided him a position of influence with those at the highest corporate levels. And, delightfully for Pete, his reputation among blacks and women was impeccable.

Within a couple of years Pete had worked out an ideal *alignment*. He had a way of engaging each constituency that allowed them to see how his actions related to results they valued. There seemed to be a 99 percent overlap between his personal definition of success and the missions and responsibilities assigned to him, and no one in the company could perform them better.

The other 19 managers receiving the same charter as Pete, but working elsewhere in the corporation, didn't fare nearly as well. Perhaps lack of know-how, perhaps enculturation in the corporation's way of doing things, or perhaps a different tolerance for conflict had made them reluctant to aggressively challenge higher-ups. With time, to a greater or lesser degree, their roles degenerated to those of commiserator and management "go-for." They always seemed to be on the defensive, trying to prove themselves rather than challenging others to be more excellent. Their weakness and low-keyed tactics made Pete's strength and accomplishments look all the more potent.

Eventually those sitting in upper corporate echelons took notice of the overall situation and decided that Pete was the role model of what they were trying to achieve. They approached Pete with an offer of a promotion if he would agree to supervise and train the other nineteen managers. Pete's first reaction was to accept, but something held him back. At the time, he didn't understand his hesitancy, so he merely used it to negotiate a sweeter deal. He would not take responsibility for the others, there were too many bad habits to overcome. But he would step up a level in his current territory and accept overall responsibility for recruitment, career planning, minority advancement, and improved managerial functioning.

Pete's promotion put him on the same level with other line managers. He became a regular member of the management team and now directly supervised three managers who were responsible for about forty professional employees and oversaw the hiring of outside consultants.

Unfortunately, at this point, his alignment fell apart and his work life became filled with aggravation. *First*, his former associates began treating him like their boss, which he was, and this severely undermined his ability to coach and openly suggest. Now his suggestions were heard as orders and his inadvertent questions were received as well-thought-out criticisms.

*Next*, his relationships with blacks and women went to pot. His elevation in the hierarchy caused him to be seen as manager rather than human rights worker and he was treated to rounds of Mau-Mauing and confrontations, as what formerly had been received as his in-group remarks were interpreted as racial and sexist slurs.

*Next*, Pete found that the added amount of time his new job required for supervision, staff meetings, and report writing reduced the time available for the internal consulting role he prized.

On top of everything else, a "screw-up" in another division involving a racial-awareness consultant set off a reactionary wave up to an executive vice-president who responded by ordering sharp cutbacks in the use of outside consultants. For Pete, this had the personal effect of cutting off sources of his support and learning and the task effect of withdrawing the quality resources needed to keep his operation competently stationed and challenging to the status-quo.

To top these disappointments, after about three months in the new job, Pete's boss called him in for a coaching session where he received word that his new peers were concerned that he was hurting his career by appearing to be such a deviant and advocate for minorities. Pete returned to his office screaming, "What the hell is going on here, these are the same jokers who wanted me promoted because I *was* such a deviant?!"

This was the last straw. Not only were his former constituents treating him like one of the "other guys" but the "other guys" were claiming that he was too much of a deviant for them.

———◆———

From our perspective Pete was caught without either a personally effective or an organizationally successful alignment. His personal viewpoint wasn't registering anywhere. Nowhere was he actively shaping reality. His alignment had become obsolete. He was in the same position his nineteen former counterparts had found themselves in when they were charged with a mission to which they could not personally relate and thus could not confidently assert an articulate point of view.

Incidentally, and no pun intended, this is not a case of the "Peter Principle." We know Pete and he's anything but a person who had been promoted above his level of competence. We believe it is just a matter of time before Pete constructs a new alignment, one that allows him to use his new job for personal expression and to further the missions he values. But until he gets realigned, the self-deliberations entailed in trying to match self-interests with what seems to be required by his job will provide him with many lonely hours of unhappiness and frustration.

Pete's story was chosen because it illustrates the active dimension of the orienting process we call alignment. It shows the importance of an individual's commitment to inner values. That Pete could succeed, both inwardly and outwardly, where nineteen others could not is a tribute to his success in finding a good match between his personal needs and interests and what he saw as needed by the job. He had an effective alignment. The nineteen others lacked an effective alignment and most of them became either *cynics* or *careerists*. The cynics converged on alignments that subordinated the organization's needs to their own interests and values. They saw management's view as constraints to be navigated around, not perspectives to be joined and possibly learned from. Conversely, the careerists adopted alignments that subordinated their personal interests and values to what they thought would score on the organization checklist. They ground out workshop after workshop, training event after training event, but without the conversations and conflicts that could budge the status quo.

The concept of alignment, and Pete's story, provides support for most people's contention that repackaging themselves to fit a particular job or role does not constitute a sell-out to the job, although to an outsider their compromises frequently appear fatal. As Pete's situation illustrates, people need to shift alignments when they change jobs or experience a new set of external demands, even though their interests, skills and values remain the same. While self-interests remain relatively constant, the form in which they are pursued and expressed must shift. How often we've seen people criticize the way their boss operates only to themselves embody much of the same behavior as they shift alignments upon moving up to the boss' level in the organization.

———————◆———————

In summary, we see the concept of alignment as a key addition to how people should be thinking about organizations. There's a level of organization residing within each individual that explains how that person does his or her job and views external organization events. If there's an external organization that determines how groups of people relate in doing work together then there's an *internal organization,* far more encompassing than an individual's personality, that determines how individuals within groups transact their business and work for the greater institutional good. Moreover, despite their lack of prominence in how people present themselves, self-interests are a dominant factor in determining what gets produced in the name of organizationally required product and how what is produced is received. And you don't need the skills of a psychoanalyst to understand these self-interests. You merely need to comprehend what an individual is trying to express personally and achieve in his or her career, and what he or she perceives as making a valuable contribution to the job. At every point personal needs and organization goals impact on one another, and it's always up in the air whether the needs of the job or the interests of the individual will swamp the other or whether a synergy of interests will evolve.

Thus *alignment* is our term for the highly personal orientation one takes to the job that must be known before we can comprehend the meaning and intent of someone's actions. Sometimes people do different things for the same reason. Sometimes people do the same thing for different reasons. Without knowing people's alignment, taking their actions on face value—even those with a direct connection to bottom-line product—leads to erroneous conclusions. The only way to comprehend what people are about is to know what they are trying to express and achieve personally and what assumptions they are making about the organizational avenues for doing so.

---

At this point we provide a guide to comprehending the personal side of an individual's orientation to the job. It's a set of questions which, when thoughtfully answered, provide a new perspective on why an individual does his or her job the way he or she does it, and why that person views organization events in a particular way. Add in the task requisites of the job, as the individual sees them, and you've got that person's alignment. Incidentally, we've had marvelous results using an abbreviated list of these questions as preparation for team-building meetings at which a boss and his or her subordinates get together for a long session to discuss opportunities for improving their work-group's effectiveness. Twenty to forty minutes each, around the group, and the edge comes off many premeeting criticisms. Instead of being programmed to fault one another for inadequacy, the discussion takes a constructive turn as participants contrast the fit between an individual's needs and talents with what participants see as the task requisites of that person's job.

---

The questions we use in seeking to understand the self-interest side of an individual's alignment fall into three categories: personal, career, and organizational. Specifically we ask questions drawn from, but not limited to, the following list.

## SELF-INTEREST QUESTIONS
### Personal

*What are you trying to prove to yourself and, very importantly, why?*

*What are you trying to prove to others? Give an instance that illustrates why and how.*

*What style of life are you trying to maintain or achieve? (Does this entail a change in income? —geography? family size? etc.)*

*Name the people who have played significant roles in your life and say what those roles were.*

*What dimensions would you like to add to your personal life and why?*

*What motto would you like to have carved on your tombstone and how do you want to be remembered by the people who are close to you?*

## Career

*What profession do you want to wind up in? (If you are an engineer and you say "management," tell why. If you are not in that profession, say how you plan to get into it.)*

*How did you, or will you, develop competency in that profession?*

*What do you want to accomplish in that profession?*

*What honor or monument would you like to have symbolize your success in that profession? Say why it would constitute a personal hallmark.*

## Organizational

*What has been your image in your organization and what would you like it to be?*

*Describe a bum-rap or overly simplistic category others
have used in describing you and tell either why you are
different now or why their statement was simplistic or
too categorical.*

*What is the next lesson you need to learn and what are
your plans for doing so?*

*What would you like to be doing two to five years out?**

*What would you like to be doing ten years out?**

While we encourage people to share perspectives generated
by these questions with work associates whom they trust, we
do not recommend that they reveal specific instances in which
self-interests played a role in determining one of their organizational actions. We don't because we fear that others, however well-intentioned, will inadvertently misuse such candor
later on. What we advocate is that each individual simply
provide associates a more valid context for viewing his or her
goals and accomplishments.

---

* Think of "doing" in terms of a specific assignment (job, position,
status) and specify it in terms of a specific role (player, coach, expert)
and how you would like to be performing it.

# SURVIVING IN THE SYSTEM | III

Part II displayed the imperfections in what may be the best system in the world. If it is the best, we contend that it is because it allows ample room for the expression of self-interests. If it has serious imperfections, we contend that these reside in the human pain and compromises in organization missions that arise from the underground way people are forced to fight in pursuing their alignments. We have attempted to expose the pervasiveness of these conflicts and to portray them as a highly understandable state of affairs, given the unique and individualistic definitions of success people seek.

Now we're ready to take our analysis one step further. In the last part we focused on motives. In this part we identify the methods people use in pursuing self-interests and explore some of the consequences of using those methods.

In Chapters 6 to 8 we present what we have identified as the three basic types of *survival tactics* people use in pursuing self-interests while resisting the controls of those who want them to operate differently. Incidentally, we call these survival tactics because, as our examples have already illustrated, today's victor in the war of meanings can easily become tomorrow's victim. "Framing," the first tactic we examine, is used when someone is "on the make," trying to assert a perspective that gets his or her contributions and orientation valued. The second, "fragmenting," is used when someone is "on the run," trying to escape an indictment that emanates from someone with a conflicting orientation. The third, "playing-it-both-ways," is used when someone is "slipping through" attempting to avoid conflict while pursuing a course that others, if they knew about it, would want to censor.

The last three chapters explore the destructive impact survival tactics can have on the individuals who use them and on the organizations in which they work. Chapter 9 describes the variety of the disorientation that takes place, Chapter 10 the extraordinary difficulties in getting reoriented once the system in which one is operating runs amuck, and Chapter 11 what people must understand before they can act differently.

# 6 | FRAMING

We've decided to begin this section on survival in the system by telling you about someone who failed to survive and showing you exactly why. It happened to Nancy, a talented, well-intentioned, and highly motivated woman hired as the education director of a large professional association.

———◆———

Three months after Nancy signed on as education director the program director quit. To everyone's dismay, it was discovered that planning had not yet begun for the national convention only six months off. Nancy and several others were called on to help. The others carefully measured their contributions, getting to them only after their other responsibilities were fulfilled. Nancy, however, recognized that someone needed to be open-endedly committed or the convention would never come off. So she voluntarily took on a leadership role which she understood would be relinquished once a new program director was hired. Of course, Nancy continued to fulfill her scheduled responsibilities as education director, including arranging regional seminars and publishing a monthly technical bulletin. While she could competently handle these, she had to put off a larger task with a less immediate deadline—editing and publishing a long-planned series of professional books.

Nancy found performing both jobs was hectic and exhausting, but wonderfully satisfying. She derived considerable satisfaction from the belief that she was shoring up a critical gap. She also got points from those working around her. They appreciated that she was new on the job and holding down two demanding assignments. They even noticed that she would do her own typing when her secretary was tied up with something important.

Nancy's stop-gap leadership freed the association's executive director to conduct a nationwide search for a new program director. Eventually he found a marvelous one, but this was only a month before the convention and too late to take the pressure off Nancy. The new program director immediately displayed the skills of a savvy organization worker—he announced that the up-coming convention would probably be a disaster but that he might be able to salvage part of it.

The convention turned out to be but a mixed success. The executive committee's disappointment with the convention triggered their built-up frustrations over a series of instances in which the staff had failed to deliver what had been promised. They were reminded of the previous program director's irresponsible departure. And Nancy's role in the convention brought to mind the delay in publishing the professional books for which she was responsible. Their publication was to have been the accomplishment that distinguished their terms in office.

At that point, there wasn't a single board member who would give Nancy the benefit of a doubt. Each attributed the convention's shortcomings to Nancy's inexperience, while attributing its successes to the new program director's last minute brilliance. As a result, Nancy's honest and humble self-presentation was interpreted as an admission of incompetence and the board called for her dismissal. Those working with Nancy, including the executive director, came forward, but their statements vouching for her contributions, sacrifice, and talents were read as after-the-fact testimonies of her amiability, not of her bottom-line accomplishments. Board members contended that even if they conceded that the convention wasn't her responsibility, which they really didn't believe, getting those books out was—and she hadn't produced.

———————◆———————

So Nancy lost while those less conscientious and more self-serving in her organization survived. She lost because board members lacked the categories for seeing her inputs, her accomplishments, and her commitments at the time she was delivering them. Why didn't they revise their perceptions when her story was told? Because like all of us they felt they had been there before. Too well they understood the omnipresence of self-interests and the ease with which people can produce self-serving rationalizations to cover over ineffective performances. After-the-fact, people can justify anything. Here was Nancy asking them to believe that she was the consummate team player attempting nothing less than to save their organization from embarrassment at their biggest media event of the year. That was a lot to swallow. The question, then, is whether Nancy could have done it differently. What might she have done so that her contributions would be valued?

———◆———

Nancy failed because she did not *frame* the situation for her survival and possible success. Before she ever started pitching in she needed to construct and market a reality that would allow others to value both her orientation and the contributions that orientation would produce. We refer to the act of constructing such a reality as *framing*.

More specifically, framing has three components: (a) a simple story that links an individual's commitments to a highly principled logic, connected to (b) the tangible products or practical consequences flowing from such a commitment, backed up by (c) the appropriateness of or authority base underlying this position. In Nancy's case, before-the-fact she would have had to present herself as: (a) the consummate team player stepping in to fill an essential organizational void, (b) out to save the organization from catastrophic embarrassment, with (c) the full sanctioning of the executive director and probably some key members of the board as well. After-the-fact Nancy could produce the first two components but not the third. She might have won a drop of grace had she produced the third, but her boss hedged. He had promised to have the books out and didn't want to take the heat. When questioned, he said, "I knew she was pitching in more than the rest of us but I figured either that she had the spare time or was involved in a convention detail which couldn't be postponed."

Framing is an activity that forces others to relate to entire structures, not just single arguments. It fixes one's position and/or contribution within a reality construction where details can be disputed but where one's basic stand is bolstered by multiple levels of impact and appears more or less unassailable. No one can count on finding others whose orientations are sufficiently similar to see the value in each view he or she advances, however, skillful framing erects an underlying structure that allows others to differ on specific points without jeopardizing the basic position on which the points are based.

---

Nowhere is the art of framing more highly developed than in the realm of politics where politicians persuasively construct frameworks that get people to reason on tracks similar to their own. This is where to see how framing works in action. For instance, look at what Senator Barry Goldwater was able to construct in only three minutes on radio spots he did on the topics of defense and welfare spending. On consecutive nights he used the same structure to support defense and attack welfare without appearing the least bit inconsistent. Consider the difficulty in opposing his position once the Senator had framed the topic.

> In supporting a strong defense budget, Senator Goldwater emphasized only the "positives." *First*, he described the security that comes from a nation's ability to actively wage war. *Second*, he talked about deterrents and the role a strong defense system plays in the United States' ability to position its interests on the world political scene. *Third*, he described the technological payoffs associated with defense research and the contribution defense spending makes to economic health. *Last*, he characterized military service as a leveling force for our country, contributing greatly to advances in civil rights, maturation of youths and the development of leaders.
> 
> The next night his assessment of welfare emphasized only the "negatives." *First*, he began by arguing that our welfare programs fail to help the people they are designed to reach. He said aid to dependent children encourages people who shouldn't to have more children and direct payments to the poor encourage poor people to remain job-

less. *Second,* he stated that welfare payments cause people who ordinarily wouldn't qualify to worsen their situation so that they receive a little less income for a lot less effort. *Third,* he took up the direct costs to taxpayers, stating that taxes spent on welfare reduce purchasing power and deprive us of higher standards of living. *Last,* he described how rising taxes erode the incentive structure of our society by discouraging the hard work and risk-taking that are at the heart of the free enterprise system that has made America great.

The strength in Goldwater's approach lies not in the facts he presents, but in the frameworks he constructs. These frameworks organize the facts into an intricate picture of reality that has diffuse and self-convenient arguments mutually reinforcing one another. For instance, it is possible for someone to disagree with the Senator by complaining "You mean to tell me that the military develops better leaders than the Peace Corps?" and "The proportion of cheating in the welfare budget is no more than the fat in the military budget or in the corporation expense accounts!" without disturbing, in the slightest, the overall persuasiveness of Senator Goldwater's position. The senator doesn't even have to reply and he's still ahead.

How does the senator's framework stack up with our criteria for framing? First, he links his viewpoint to a highly principled logic, that of doing what's needed to build a strong and greater America. Second, he explains the benefits accruing from his position, both short and long term. He says strong defense gives us the immediate ability to defend interests worldwide and, on five separate points, reinforces the very structure that makes America great. He challenges welfare spending by castigating the system for producing results that run counter to its intent and calls attention to at least four areas in which welfare undermines the American way. *Third,* listening to his innuendos and voice tone makes it crystal clear that his is not a single voice. He speaks out from his recognized position as trusted spokesman for the conservative American tradition.

Of course Senator Goldwater is a master, and most framing takes place with a more moderate degree of expertise. To illustrate, let's turn to a more typical example taken from the annals of a small manufacturing firm.

———————————◆———————————

At the point we enter the scene, the personnel manager has just been fired and hourly workers are getting ready to mount their annual spring vote on unionization. The top managers are discussing the need both for a replacement and for a strategy that communicates management's good will toward workers.

GEORGE — (referring to the hourly workers) Seems to me there are two ways to go. We can either bribe them by increasing wages across the board or find a way to show them that we are responsive to their concerns.

STEVE — There's no current problem with wages, our salary administrator just gave us the green light. My foreman says the hourly want assurances that we won't "hard-line" them when their complaints get beyond kicking over our unwillingness to sponsor a bowling league.

CAROL — Sounds to me like they want to know that there's someone who will take a stand for them.

GEORGE — That's exactly it. We don't need just another personnel guy, we need an *in-house* employee advocate.

STEVE — You mean, as contrasted with an *out-house* union? Yuk, yuk.

BART — Seriously, I like Carol's idea too. What if we make Ken the personnel manager, they trust him, and charge him with being the employees' advocate.

MEL — How would that work?

BART — Well, Ken knows the paper work, and he's done hiring. What we need is an angle for his being their man and not ours.

CAROL — But he is ours.

STEVE — He doesn't have to be. Let's strip the personnel manager's decision-making role, not on rinky dink issues like fixing the price of the coffee machine, but on big things like salary schedules and leave and vacation policy. Give him the job of worker-management go-between.

BART — I think you're almost there but that's not quite it. If you make Ken a go-between, it won't take five minutes before they think he's playing a double role. I think he ought to be their advisor, consultant, clarifier, but that they ought to hold their own individual conversations with us. When someone or some group has a gripe let them test it out on Ken and then step forward themselves.

MEL — I think you've got it. Somebody ought to get Ken in here before we go too far in hammering out the fine points.

Somebody did get Ken and the personnel manager's mission was imaginatively conceptualized as someone who would help employees to represent their interests to management and to get fair consideration for what they propose. At first it was an extremely difficult role for Ken to play because he'd been schooled to see things through managerial eyes. Eventually Ken adapted. He had to go beyond the self-image of seeing himself as ducking his "managerial" duty to be a decision maker in order to represent employee interests. It even took some adapting by the other managers, but fortunately most of them were there when Ken's mission was being formulated.

---

Let's reflect this example against the three framing criteria.

*First, the overarching logic* — the company needs an employee advocacy system that replaces the employees' need for a union.

*Second, connected to practical outcomes* — the company gets an up-stream barometer for sensing employee concerns and employees develop an open communication channel to management.

*Third, outcomes backed up by a legitimate authority* — this scheme was thought up in a conversation in which most of the managers who would have to absorb the challenges and confrontations marshalled by Ken's efforts participated.

Is it working? It's seven months later and it seems to be. There wasn't even a vote last spring and the overtime management dreads is down.

---

Lest the reader jump to the conclusion that framing is synonymous with winning, examine with us first the rise and then the fall of one of the truly great "framers" of any age—Robert Strange McNamara. For a while McNamara's framing skills enabled him to do what no man has been able to do before or since. He took command of the world's largest organization, the United States Department of Defense, and made his concerns the central reality orienting that department's operations.

In 1960, when McNamara assumed the job of Secretary of Defense he inherited an organization that most experts considered to be irretrievably out of control. Yet within sixty days following his arrival at the Pentagon, and for the four years preceding the escalation of the Viet Nam War, McNamara accomplished the impossible. He framed the questions that brought the generals under control.

McNamara accomplished this by mastering data that made it possible for him to singlehandedly face down all opposition, whether it came from Pentagon generals, senators and congressmen or other members of the Kennedy-Johnson cabinets. Who among those who witnessed his appearances before the highly suspicious Congressional Armed Services Subcommittee can forget McNamara's cool, detached, and analytic recitations of the intimate details associated with virtually every program within his department. Under his leadership, a shift was made in the strategic orientation of the defense program from "all-out deterrent" to "balanced and flexible response."

McNamara's story, his overarching logic, was simple and to the point. He was there to bring modern management practices to a military that was disciplined and efficient in combat but undisciplined and inefficient in administration. Simply stated, his were the techniques of systems analysis. Their power was based on the requirement that any program or operational unit must, on the front end, define its mission in terms that could be objectively stated and, most importantly, be measured.

The rules of the game were straightforward. If you didn't formulate your projects in cost benefit calculus, with alternatives listed, then you didn't get a hearing from McNamara. And McNamara had his own "whiz kids," high-powered staff analysts, who were only too happy to fill the void with their own analyses whenever someone failed to present his. The result was that McNamara was never at a loss for a well-formulated position on a critical issue.

Why was the military willing to play a game they couldn't control? At first they had no choice. To refuse would mean bucking the conventional wisdom of three decades which argued that tough-minded private sector practices were needed to wrest inept and unresponsive bureaucracies from the hands of the careerists. What's more, there had been growing public concern over a military running out of control, symbolized by the early warning episode in which Truman had to replace an out-of-control general in Korea named MacArthur.

So it was that into 1964 McNamara reigned supreme, not only in the Department of Defense but also as one of Lyndon Johnson's most trusted cabinet advisors. While McNamara may not have been successful in completely cutting off military "end runs" to Congress, even his most vocal critics readily conceded that it was McNamara's agenda—his questions and his concerns—that occupied center stage at the Pentagon from 1960 to 1964. How was it possible, then, that less than four years later McNamara was removed from office with the whole country after his skin. Not only was he being harassed and taunted by the "doves" as the architect of the disastrous Viet Nam strategy but, by the end of his term, was being contemptuously regarded and openly ridiculed by the military as weak and ineffectual. What happened to McNamara's vaunted systems analysis and his ability to monitor events and control the war?

At the end, McNamara's strength became his weakness. In the early years he had been able to stay in control by demanding that all communications be structured to fit within his picture of "objective" reality. But the military caught on and were able to turn McNamara's logic to their own advantage. They began to "interact" with the numbers of "body counts," "kill ratios," and "bombing strikes" which McNamara received and absorbed into his computer-like brain for analysis. One can picture McNamara on one of his later trips to Viet Nam being briefed by bright young military officers armed with flip charts and the figures necessary to demonstrate how well the war was going while the surrounding countryside was enduring a dramatically different fate.

Eventually members of McNamara's own staff caught on.

They began to sense that "statistical reality" and the actual progress of the war were at sharp odds, but they found Mc-Namara a hard man to reach. They lacked the "hard data" to make their case. McNamara seemed swallowed up by his own logic. While his early successes had been the result of getting the world around him to buy into his way of framing reality, his downfall came in believing that *his* reality was the actual reality.

---

In summary, we have seen that framing is the survival tactic used to create self-convenient organizational reality and that it works by presenting others with an interlocking set of appeals to advance lofty ideals, to pursue practical outcomes, and to support established authority. The story of Nancy illustrates how, in the absence of framing, an otherwise effective contribution can go unrecognized. The speeches of Senator Goldwater illustrate the difficulty in countering a point of view that has been anchored with effective framing. The example in which a group of managers created a new personnel mission depicts how framing can be the result of a relatively simple effort and how, when effectively done, it provides the roadmap necessary for getting others to appreciate and value someone's efforts. And finally, the history of Robert Mc-Namara was resurrected to demonstrate the danger of getting so wrapped up with the self-convenient way you construct reality, made possible through the artful use of framing, that you begin to accept your own view of reality as absolute objectivity.

Now we are ready to move on to describe the second survival tactic—fragmenting. Whereas framing is the tactic people use in aggressively moving into a void to get their point of view or contribution valued, fragmenting is the tactic people use when they are on the receiving end of a reality that was constructed without their best interests in mind.

# 7 | FRAGMENTING

A boss screams up and down the halls about the amount of overtime your department is working, neglecting that you have stretched yourself to the breaking point by staffing thin in order to save the company thousands of dollars a month and glossing over the fact that it was an attempt to meet the priority dates specified in his latest directive that put you over the standard budget for overtime.

A subordinate whose head you've been holding above water for months while he went through the throes of a divorce appropriately reads your last criticism as the signal that you're about to toughen up and decides to beat you to the punch by requesting a transfer on the grounds that your poor management is the primary cause of his nonperformance.

A task force colleague takes exception that you scheduled an important meeting at a time she could not attend after you had already scheduled two previous meetings at ungodly times to suit her convenience and she never showed.

———————◆———————

Familiar dilemmas? How do you survive on the receiving end of a reality that was framed with someone else's best interests in mind? What do you do when held to an absolute definition of commitment and responsibility which bears little relation to your contributions or overall goals?

Admittedly we have cited extreme examples, but they are indicative of the type of situation that one can expect to encounter on a daily basis. Each finds someone confronting you with a reality chosen for its convenience to them rather than its relevance to what concerns you. It's as if the "framer" assumes that his or her interests should be center stage for you at all times and that there aren't other constituencies, perspectives and survival needs that you simultaneously must take into account.

———————◆———————

Basically, there are two ways to deal with such situations. Either one can depict the totality and complexity of his or her involvements, or one can present a version of the truth that best represents his or her projects in the face of the framer's concerns. And since there's usually little incentive for the framer to examine things from the respondent's standpoint, the second response is the one that is usually chosen. The respondent proceeds to split the truth into pieces which he or she dispenses at self-convenient times. We call this type of schism *fragmenting* because reality is split up in such a way that although every piece or fragment is more or less true, the totality is misleading.

*Fragmenting* is the survival tactic which allows people to pursue self-interests in a world that often does not acknowledge the legitimacy of such interests and in which others approach us as if they have the right to expect that we be immediately responsive to issues which are of priority concern to them. To the boss who screams about overtime one fragments by responding, "I assumed that your recent directive stressing preferential treatment for our big customers implied a variance in my overtime budget." To those listening to the subordinate covering over nonperformance one fragments by smiling confidently and saying, "I'm not surprised Jim felt things were out of control, but I think if you were to examine the situation closely you'd find that his people have been looking to me for their primary guidance for months now." And to the colleague upset about her exclusion from an important meeting one fragments by apologetically stating, "My secretary must have misunderstood about your availability because I distinctly told her to find a time when *all* the key players could attend."

Inconsistency is the trademark of fragmenting. People tell different stories to different listeners; they define the responsibilities and obligations associated with their roles differently at different times; they promise one set of standards in selling what they are about to do and use a different set of standards in justifying what they just did; and they send out messages which are internally inconsistent. Moreover, much of this is done without conscious deception intended. But regardless of what is intended there is deception—subtleties are added, nuances emphasized, details omitted, and inconsistency reigns throughout.

Fragmenting seems to be the only way to cope in a society

in which increasing numbers of people with varied interests see themselves having a stake in what we do and how it gets done. In fact, each day more and more of us wake up to find ourselves in a fishbowl, watched and questioned even by people who appear to have only the remotest interest in what we are trying to achieve.

Unfortunately, the more people with different interests to whom we answer, the more difficult it becomes to formulate statements that accurately and candidly represent our point of view. The questions produced by diverse interests can make even our simplest story sound unintelligible. Others seldom bother with the overall complexity of what we've set out to do. They merely want us to address their concerns. "Don't bother with all that background, answer our questions!" They expect straightforward, simply phrased answers which we don't seem able to provide. For one thing, we are busy piecing what they ask us into the full complex of issues involved in our actions, and for another, we first have to decode their questions and pretest our answers against what we think they want to hear. Moreover, our answers must fit with what we have told or will tell others with competing orientations so that candor and rapport with one person or group does not mean trouble with another.

Thus, we boggle at answering the simplest questions and have our IQs reduced by 50 points in the minds of almost everyone listening to us. We're in the ridiculous position of figuring out an ingenious response, one that responds to five or six interests at once, to a question which may pose us with an impossible personal predicament, while others view our answers as simplistic and representative of a stereotypical thinker.

Now most of those to whom we will eventually have to answer have not yet given much conscious thought to us—and they won't until some event signals that it's our turn in the fishbowl. But when this happens, will their case ever come together fast. Like a turn of a kaleidoscope, all their past experiences with us, particularly the problematic ones, will come into a focus that unfairly emphasizes the flaws in what we've been about. Everyone knows yesterday's actions look inadequate in the face of today's knowledge, but this won't deter our questioners. Even their complicity in our shortsightedness will be overshadowed by what they now want to tell us we did wrong. Even-handed analysis goes out the window; it's our turn to answer the questions. And oh, those questions! It's as if each one were consciously designed to make us look inadequate.

For example, consider what, of all people, public accountants face today. For years they were just like the rest of us, cruising along without much scrutiny. In fact, they were among the most highly respected and trusted professional groups in our society. Until recently, when a problem arose, the public was inclined to grant public accountants the credibility of bankers. Today accountants get no such grace.

At this point, we believe it worthwhile to stop and consider in detail what public accountants are facing. It's a graphic example of how good framing begets excellent fragmenting. Here we caution those readers who are inclined to skip, perhaps thinking that there's nothing more dull than an accountant, to forego your impulse and stick with us, for this example illustrates the way artful fragmenting can stave off the most devastating of criticisms.

### Public Accountants

In the late 1920s when the financial community went sour, the big question was, "How to restore investor confidence?" To oversimplify somewhat, the eventual solution had two parts. First, the government would insure bank savings, and second, public accountants would provide safeguards for stock-market investors by independently reviewing the books of each publicly held company as well as management's statements of how their company was doing. In this way investors could trust the financial information offered to them by management and confidence in the stockmarket would be restored. Led by public accountants, and with the help of a few other private and governmental review boards such as the Securities and Exchange Commission (SEC), the United States financial community regrouped and established a credibility second to none in the world.

We're not sure whether any specific event triggered the shift in the kaleidoscopes used in viewing public accountants or whether the low level suspicions each profession evokes in the groups it impacts reached some critical mass, but suddenly the tough-to-answer "simple" questions that signify a framer's ire started pouring in. Suddenly, daily practices that had never before evoked serious concern came under intense scrutiny. Consider some of what's being asked of public accountants today and then let us show you the kinds of answers made possible by skillful fragmenting. Each question comes with a "when did you stop beating your wife?" flavor but each fragmented answer keeps the accountants a step ahead of their critics.

*Stockholders* who studied the annual report of the Penn Central Railroad and bought in after the railroad was doomed, ask: "How could you give a bill-of-health in December to a company that went bankrupt the following July?"

*Public interest groups,* such as the National Council of Churches, who wonder how million dollar bribes eluded detection by the public accountants at Lockheed who in one year spent 25,000 hours combing through the company's books, ask: "How do you account for your signature on financial reports which are cover-ups for illegal slush funds and bribes?"

*University professors,* criticizing the consulting and tax businesses public accountants run on the side as "an accommodation to our clients" and which accounts for up to 40 percent of their income, ask: "How can you 'advertise an independent, skeptical, arm's length relationship with management' when the very people who hire and fire you are the people you're supposed to be investigating?"

*Managers,* who are particularly sensitive to ties public accountants have to the past and their reluctance to endorse contemporary accounting procedures that could provide a more valid presentation of how well the company is doing, ask: "How can you call us your clients, charge us exorbitant fees, and then put us in a straightjacket by forcing us to use accounting practices that make it impossible to get the most adventurous part of our story across?"

*Company accountants,* who spend enormous time providing data and interpretations for public accountants whose job is to catch them up short, ask: "How can you run a business that depends on our wholehearted cooperation when the information we provide is used against us?"

*SEC lawyers,* who can't understand how the public accountants avoided complicity in frauds involving as much as $2 billion in bogus insurance at Equity Funding, ask: "Why do you insist on putting your reports in a difficult to interpret form that makes it easy for some stock brokers and financial analysts to mislead the public?"

*Financial analysts,* who have in mind shenanigans such as those exposed at Mattel when early signs of a disastrous year were concealed from stockholders by declaring first, second, and third quarter profits while management scurried unsuccessfully to recoup, ask: "How much longer are you going to stand pat in your refusal to sign quarterly statements while companies exploit us by directing profits to quarters that suit their interests?"

*And the general public,* who believes public accountants have access to all important financial information and should lead the way in putting business on a higher plane, ask: "Can't you guys do a better job of guaranteeing our investments and blowing the whistle on fraudulent business practices?"

These aren't all the people with questions nor all their complaints, but they give the general idea. At face value each group of challengers seems to have a legitimate beef. How can the public accountants survive such devastating criticisms?

At first, public accountants tried ignoring the criticisms, but this only seemed to bring out more critics who appeared more persistent than ever in voicing their challenges. Then they tried to dispute the criticisms which brought them to their critics' structure where they found, as we have already seen, that winning points came at the expense of losing battles and that over the long haul this tactic did them no good. Of course, they easily understood the problems associated with accepting the validity of even one criticism. Doing so would either subject them to endless litigation or would be tantamount to admitting that they have assumed a societal role which they can no longer perform.

Fragmenting bailed the accountants out. It didn't win them the war but it does seem to be buying them another day. Despite all the "I've got ya!" criticisms, public accountants continue to pull down gigantic six-figure salaries while operating more or less as they always have. And in terms of our study it's enlightening to examine the specific statements they made, all in the spirit of fragmenting, which today allows them to hold their critics off.

---

For example, consider the public accountants' response to stockholders of the Penn Central Railroad who asked, "How could you give a bill-of-health in December to a company that went bankrupt the following July?" To this they replied, "We conducted our audit in the professional manner set forth in the standards dictated by our profession." This statement is simply ingenious, it combines three kinds of fragmenting. *First*, it's not the fault of the public accountants who conducted the audit and wrote it up. It's their profession's. *Second*, when confronted on their outputs, they respond with inputs. The implications are, "We did it right, we can't help it that investors got burned." *Third*, they imply that professional standards are meant to protect, would you believe, professionals from the public—not the public from the professionals.

Let's examine another one. How do public accountants defend carrying on lucrative consulting practices with the very clients they are supposed to be investigating? Again they invoke professionalism. They say, "It makes no difference that 40 percent of our revenues come from providing consulting and tax services to our clients, since we take a professional oath of independence and pride ourselves on our integrity." Here fragmenting takes place by their invoking different standards for different folks. On one hand they say, "You can trust us to conduct an impartial audit even though a client's displeasure could cost us income." On the other hand, there isn't a public accountant alive who could tolerate an analogous management situation, say, where the same corporate officer is responsible both for disbursing large sums of money and for accounting how the money was used. Let's face it, most accountants wouldn't even trust their mothers to straddle this kind of situation. Yet, from their response, this is exactly what they are asking us to believe they can handle.

How do public accountants account for their signature on reports that cover over illegal slush funds and bribes? To this they respond, "The payments weren't large enough to be detected by our routine search procedures. After all, you wouldn't want us spending thousands of dollars to investigate a $100 shortage in pencils and erasers." Fragmenting again, this time their story-splitting results from what they're not saying. They want us to understand that the self-confessed $35 million in illegal overseas payments coming out of Lockheed in less than four years wasn't large enough for them to detect. Whom are they kidding? How about the managers who, knowing their firm's auditors didn't investigate shortages of less than $25,000, managed to salt away $10 million using a "laundering mill" in the Bahamas—in $24,000 increments of course.

What about public accountants' refusal to dignify the accuracy of quarterly earnings statements with their signature? Is this not a place where they resisted fragmenting, after all getting into the quarterly reporting business would appreciably boost their income? They did put up a genuine fight but eventually said, "We have to go along with the SEC ruling requiring our participation despite the fact that we fear such involvement will lead unsophisticated investors to attach yet higher levels of meaning and precision to what are no more than rough estimates." Here they split their story by going along with a position that, if it blows up on them, they can later claim they were forced into. In this context they don't talk about other SEC rulings which they successfully fought, but which they do refer to at other times when it suits their interests.

Lastly, how do public accountants respond to clients who complain about not being allowed to use accounting practices which favorably and fairly represent their story, despite the fact that they are footing the bill? To this they respond, "Don't worry, we're on your side. We understand the pressures you people are under but you've got to realize that there are dark forces out there which aren't as sympathetic as we. If we're coming on strong it's because the SEC is breathing down our neck and there are zealots in Congress who would like to see us really rat on you." Here the public accountants' fragmenting concerns the image they are attempting to portray. They are trying to come off as the least bad guys around while keeping quiet about the fact that the efficiency of their operations goes to pot the moment management begins to treat them like informers or adversaries. They realize the grave trouble they are in, unable to do their job, once they lose the wholehearted cooperation of management.

———————◆———————

All of the public accountants' responses entail self-serving inconsistencies, although they themselves hardly recognize this. They sense enough that's self-serving in how their critics approach them that they are able to rationalize what they do in the service of protecting their own interests. Each response represents but a part of their story—a part that is packaged one way for one critic, another for a second, and so on, without much deception intended. Certainly they don't give the SEC the same rendition they give their clients. Some of their responses indicate a willingness to change. But what they are willing to change is cosmetic. Their responses are aimed at keeping critics away from that which is fundamentally self-beneficial about their participation. In their case what's fundamental is the huge salaries orienting their practice, which have become the goals of younger people trying to make it within the profession, and the arbitrariness that underlies the precise figures they use in portraying financial "facts." In one sense, public accountants tell the public all. There's a good deal of openness about the salary potential which motivates large accounting firms to become larger and high visibility to the disclaimers which accompany every "fact" they publish. But in a deeper sense, nothing changes. The use of fragmentation allows public accountants to pursue their self-interests while feigning responsiveness to their critics' needs.

So the public accountants buy themselves another day. That, incidentally, is all that can be accomplished through fragmentation—you buy yourself one day at a time. Their critics don't seem interested in hearing the whole story, and the public accountants are not making much of an effort to get it across. But the critics aren't going to give up that easily. They know something is wrong and are increasingly frustrated that they can't pin the public accountants down. If nothing else, a deep sense of frustration will keep public accountants on their minds.

Even when they hold their critics off, the public accountants are not home free. The type of fragmenting that successfully keeps one's critics away comes at a high cost—disorientation. People become so preoccupied with the other person's categories and logic that their actions easily become disconnected from the functions they set out to perform. Certainly this is the case with the public accountants who seem to give away their birthright each time out. There is no way that they can today call themselves "independent and impartial arbitors of financial value," as their mandate dictates.

# 8 | PLAYING IT
    BOTH WAYS

"Stock car driver Darrell Waltrip said it after being dis-
qualified from a qualifying position in the Daytona 500 because of an illegal speed-boosting system: 'If you don't
cheat, you look like an idiot. If you do it and don't get
caught, you look like a hero. If you do it and get caught,
you look like a dope. Put me in the category where I be-
long.' " [*Los Angeles Times*, February 14, 1976]

Some contend that winning in the organizational world requires cheating, where the naive look like idiots and the un-
lucky like dopes. On the face of it this seems like an extreme

view and no doubt depends on what one means by cheating. Nevertheless, given what we see going on today, winning seems to require a good deal of hiding, and survival often depends on an ability to cheat. Let us explain.

If we took the time to list everything others expect, most of us would find that we've got an impossible job. Then if we added everything *we* want to do that's not on the first list, we'd see ourselves in yet a worse mess. Stepping back, the dilemma is obvious. We're finite people, capable of only so much, living in a system in which people with diverse interests expect us to say yes to their requests and to embrace their viewpoints, knowing that any honest attempt to please all will prove immobilizing and any direct attempt to extricate ourselves from ill-conceived expectations will lead to conflict. Good Old Joe who strives to be all things to all people is known as the "corporate sponge," and Tough-Minded Ed who takes the trouble to clarify misexpectations and differences is known as a "sonofabitch."

We don't have to look beyond our own situation at the university to come up with an illustration of how impossible jobs become once we pay serious attention to the varied commitments contained in other people's conceptions of what we ought to do. As professors there are at least four areas in which someone important expects us to open-endedly commit—research, teaching, university administration, and professional service. And within each of these areas there are a variety of constituencies expecting different types of outputs. For instance, our research is under constant scrutiny by scholars who want us to build on a tradition of philosophy and scholarly logic, by practical thinkers who want us to present clear explanations of the real life implications of what we know, and by research methodologists who want our findings grounded in empiricism and experimental rigor. No angle or approach pleases all, and no amount pleases anyone. What's more, making an impact requires that one choose a direction, assert him

or herself, and incur the disfavor of those who have chosen to
emphasize the other directions. In the abstract this dilemma
is understandable to everyone. But in the particular, most professors find themselves the target of criticism and deceitful
sniping by colleagues who see them holding commitments
that fail to complement their own.

---

*Playing-it-both-ways* is the name we give to the survival tactic
most people use when in the company of others whose commitments and pursuits differ from their own. It's a particular
brand of fragmenting that has individuals playing up the illusion that their commitments are sufficiently broad to encompass those which others embrace. While fragmenting is a response aimed at holding off people with different realities,
playing-it-both-ways is a response that pays lip-service to what
others are about while the individual conducts business as
usual. It's a response that recognizes that there's no payoff in
confronting others on their undervaluing and misconceptions,
and acknowledges that it's impossible to please everyone. Thus
playing-it-both-ways allows individuals to protect themselves
by keeping different concepts of output and different and limited areas of commitment from public recognition. It's a particular use of fragmenting that finds individuals passively representing their commitments and responsibilities in one way
in one group at one moment and in a different way in another
group at another moment, all with the intent of avoiding un-
productive conflicts.

Playing-it-both-ways starts at the top. At our university, it's
the president who invokes this tactic every time he goes before
the regents and the legislature. With these groups he talks as
if the primary product of the university is quality classroom
education. He knows this is the story that produces the most
funds. But he gives the university story a different slant when
communicating with the academic community. Here he em-

phasizes research. He knows better than to say anything that can be used against him when the inevitable takes place and the winner of the university teaching award is fired for lack of "scholarly research." The point is that the president (and we don't have to name him because his successor will do the same) feels the need to present the image that gets him the most mileage at the moment. And when some member of the legislature or regents confronts him on this discrepancy in his support of teaching excellence, the president is well situated to play-it-both-ways by citing all the innovative teaching efforts under way. But let one of these efforts get attacked for being more vocational than academic by a watchdog committee of faculty scholars, and he and his entire office turn mute.

There's nothing inherently sinister about playing-it-both-ways. It's often a necessary step in developing the type of control one needs in order to pursue important projects and eliminate accountability on dimensions that don't relate to the mainstream of what one is trying to accomplish. In fact it's in the spirit of performing real missions and producing accomplishment that most people resort to playing-it-both-ways, usually with hardly a moment's hesitation or the intention to deceive. To illustrate, allow us to make a big deal out of a simple, but very symbolic, interchange that took place between employee representatives and the manufacturing manager of a good-sized firm.

---

A little background is needed to place this conversation.

In an effort to maintain sensitivity to employee concerns, management had recently convened a bi-monthly "communications" meeting which was attended by elected employee representatives and a selection of managers. The purpose was to facilitate communications between the front-office and operations in the plant. The particular exchange that caught our interest was not at all unusual, which is why it constitutes a marvelous example of playing-it-both-ways.

It happened while employee representatives were criticizing the conduct of first-level foremen and, in particular, the inability of most to listen to and display respect for employee concerns. In response, the manufacturing manager jumped to his feet asking for the names of the foremen who were responsible for these problems and suggestions for remedying this unfortunate state of affairs.

This exchange graphically illustrates a basic aspect of playing-it-both-ways: people act to minimize their accountability for what others find displeasing while maximizing someone else's. In complaining about foremen, employee representatives were able to establish credibility with one another as well as with their constituencies and, without risking retaliation, nail the foremen they were out to get, all in the interest of increasing profitability for the firm. They even went so far as to couch specific comments with, "I'd be the last guy to gun down someone who isn't here but . . ." Nowhere in their complaints was there any hint of what employees themselves must do differently for their relationships with the foreman to improve.

If you think the employees played-it-both-ways, look how the manufacturing manager presented himself. Here comes Mr. Good-Guy to the rescue—he takes no responsibility for what went wrong and now that he knows the problem, he'll fix it. What's more, by asking for employee ideas for how to place controls on foremen, he gives the impression that he would have curbed this situation sooner if only he had known about it. Like the complaining employees, nowhere in his response is there any hint that he played a role in producing this problem—not that the problem was ever specified.

This example allows us to delve deeper into the structure of playing-it-both-ways, and keep in mind that it was a relatively innocuous exchange that we started with. Playing-it-both-ways allows an individual to give the illusion that his concerns mirror those of others in at least four different ways:

1. By addressing function but delivering form.

2. By professing open-ended commitment while delivering something more finite.

3. By representing inputs as outputs.

4. By establishing minimal personal accountability for one-self and one's fellow travellers while establishing maximum accountability for others.

Of course, not every playing-it-both-ways conversation accomplishes all these functions, but let's examine how they were accomplished in this example.

———————◆———————

Where do we see someone addressing function but delivering form? That's easy. The big boss left the meeting giving the appearance that he would get to the heart of the problem by having a serious discussion with those who supervise the foremen. At no time during the meeting did he even imply that it was he who had lackadaisically allowed this situation to exist for years or that it was his job to train foremen to supervise less autocratically. He then loaded the responsibility for getting rid of the complaint, not the problem, on those who supervise foremen. He told them to wise up the foremen and to quietly put the screws to employee troublemakers.

Where do we see someone professing boundless commitments while delivering something much more finite? A couple of employee representatives easily accomplished this. Among the so-called guilty foremen were two they had argued with repeatedly over judgments that they were not yet qualified to be paid the top of the rate scale of their jobs. In the statesman-like guise of improving overall organization effectiveness, they had worked a personal gripe.

Where do we see someone representing inputs as outputs? From our perspective the big boss of manufacturing qualifies for this. He indicates a strong identification with the outcome of employee/foremen relationships but focuses on what has to be an input, the enhancement of his image with employees. His behind-the-scenes actions convinced us that when neces-sary, he would cite the "serious conversations" held as evi-dence that he was doing everything possible to bring the fore-men under control.

We've already touched on the fourth element of playing-it-both-ways: minimizing personal accountability for oneself and cohorts while establishing maximum accountability for others. By chance this element was brought into the open in the next meeting when the minutes were being read and the situation updated. A manager who had missed the previous meeting half-jokingly challenged, "Sounds just like all the meetings I attend where inevitably the only guys who care are the group in the room and the troublemakers are the ones who didn't at-tend." Uh oh, caught red-handed blaming the foremen who weren't there to defend themselves. Now what do the em-ployee representatives do? This is when what we'd call *cheat-ing* often takes place. Up until now, everyone was interacting as they usually do, posturing themselves so as to protect against being held accountable on dimensions on which they could not stand to be evaluated. But what does one do once the collusion is penetrated and the questions that can divulge ac-tual commitments and perspectives begin to come in? Do the players publicly admit that they're less committed than they've been portraying themselves as being and that they've gone along with an overstated concept of responsibility? Or do they *cheat*—back-fill, stonewall, and do whatever is needed to cover up? Usually cheating only takes place when one or both of the parties is so threatened by what might be disclosed that they lose track that the other is likewise guilty of misrepresentation.

———————◆———————

In this case the big boss stonewalled and the employee representatives got honest by stating that some employees didn't really try very hard and that most were afraid to give critical feedback to a peer. Fortunately for the employees, the constant threat of unionization tempered the big boss's reaction and there were no reprisals. Nevertheless, an opportunity to improve organization effectiveness was lost, because complaints about foremen were decoded as another instance of how some hourly employees try to avoid responsibility and pass the buck.

Don't think the big boss got off scot-free. He was caught but not confronted. No one who attended either meeting thinks he played it straight, although he, as is frequently the case, thinks he got away with one. Unlike popular belief, people seldom really get away with playing-it-both-ways; they merely don't get confronted very often. Those who make fun of psychiatrists and then urgently call them in the middle of the night when someone in their family needs help don't really put one over. The supervisor who writes a piercing evaluation of a subordinate and then portrays himself as the good guy by concluding with ". . . and I've instructed him to seek *me* out for support and counseling whenever things get rough," doesn't fool anyone. The executive who splits her operation into "profit centers" and then starts issuing directives telling managers what inputs they should and should not make isn't really convincing in her assertion that she's promoting autonomy. The Pentagon colonel who retires and then, after a time period specified by law, goes to work for the very contractors to whom he awarded a multimillion dollar contract doesn't find many of us believing that he was hired for his technical competence. And the professor who tells his students that he genuinely desires to meet with them and then places a secretary and a very busy appointment book between himself and the students is accurately categorized.

Few of these instances are challenged. Each of them is clocked and, if you will, becomes a polluting force in the environments of modern organizations. Inevitably this pollution affects each of us. It contributes to the schizophrenic mentality of "this is what I have to do to cope, because all the people I'm working with operate this way." And it's all in the service of trying to act consistently with the commitments one believes in and to exercise a brand of responsibility that makes sense.

---

In sum, playing-it-both-ways is a double-edged sword. It does allow people to cope with the problem of operating within an organization where one cannot, before the fact, expect others to share or even respect the definitions of commitment and responsibility that give rise to what he or she thinks and does. But, as our examples have shown, playing-it-both-ways also comes with some costs. First, people don't fool all the people they think they are fooling. Second, even when they do fool them, their duplicitous behavior makes them active contributors to the ever-escalating level of inauthenticity taking place in organizations today. Third, calling someone on their inauthenticity creates the conditions under which people find it necessary to cheat. Fourth, playing-it-both-ways makes one an inadvertent participant in artificially controlling, rather than influencing, someone else's picture of reality so that personal success comes at the expense of multiple perspectives for others in the organization. And fifth, because cheating successfully gets people through difficult situations, it drains their incentive for sticking with a dilemma to constructively engage others on their discrepant definitions of commitment and output. The latter point is particularly important. As long as people can rationalize playing-it-both-ways on the grounds that the guys they are doing it to are doing it to them, they lose their incentive for seeking alternatives and have more reason than ever to continue playing-it-both-ways.

# 9 | DISORIENTATION

Disorientation is the inevitable consequence of framing, fragmenting, and playing-it-both-ways. An indiscernible line gets crossed and an individual's behavior becomes disconnected from the commitments he or she pursues. While individuals are able to survive, their organizational pursuits can take a perverse twist. Form begins to replace function and careerism begins to squeeze out institutional responsiveness and vitality. How else can we explain organizational absurdities such as the following?

- The Catholic teaching order where Brothers take life-long vows of poverty, chastity and obedience in the name of teaching the poor and wind up primarily running military academies for the rich in order to meet expenses.

- The Toll Bridge Authority that for years functioned with the costs of operating toll booths exceeding toll booth collections.

- The West Point Commandant who used the occasion of the second major cheating scandal in twenty years, this one involving over a third of the freshman class and prompting a congressional investigation, to claim that its discovery was proof that the honor system was alive and faring well.

- The San Francisco Water Department's appeal for users to flush their toilets two extra times a day in the height of a severe drought because an earlier appeal for conservation reduced revenues to the point where income was not meeting fixed costs.

Each of these instances exemplifies how form—the need to replicate the structures of the extant order—becomes rigidified to the point where it becomes disconnected from the function it was designed to serve. The form of running schools got disconnected from the function of serving the poor; the form of operating toll booths got disconnected from the function of generating revenues to support toll bridge maintenance; the form of the honor system got disconnected from the function of building moral character; and the form of the Water Department's rate structure got away from the function of conserving water. In each case it took a crisis to alert people to the idiocy involved. It took young Brothers' forsaking their vows in droves for the community service jobs in the ghetto; it took a new councilman "on the make" digging into the Toll Authority's budget; it took public outrage at the career harm being perpetrated upon young cadets; and it took a press that was only too happy to make the Water Department the laughing stock of the West.

———————◆———————

Now we'd like to peel back the wrapper a bit more to reveal the variety of disorientation that takes place in the daily lives of ordinary people which we attribute directly to the survival tactics they are forced to use. Ironically our first example is taken from a management classroom in which a group of students were studying the disorientation that befell Robert Mc-Namara.

Entering the classroom we find the professor upset with the written assignments students turned in on a management case taken from David Halberstam's *The Best and The Brightest,* called "The Programming of Robert Mc-Namara." Barely containing his frustration the professor says, "Spend fifteen minutes writing down the *personally* important lessons this case holds for you. Don't worry about what I'm going to think. I won't grade it."

As it turned out, what students produced in this spontaneous ungraded exercise proved to have far more insight than what they had produced in days of work on the original graded assignment. It appeared that their perceptions of what was needed to earn a high mark had subverted a display of their real understanding.

In their graded analysis most students evaluated hypercritically without any personal identification with the case. They talked as if all that was missing from the Defense Department's management was a higher level of intelligence and a more accurate information system. To their credit, students saw the link between McNamara's rational approach to management and what our culture generally considers to be "strong leadership." However, their analysis fell short of questioning how a strong leader like McNamara could have gotten himself so thoroughly exploited by the military.

The second time through, against a framework of writing what they judged to be personally relevant, their answers were full of the personal issues which McNamara had overlooked and which they judged to be the crux of his difficulties. They described contradictions between McNamara's zealous commitment to "objectivity" and the subjective factors underlying his decisions. Many could specify how the generals had taken control of the war by learning to use McNamara's highly analytical approach in the service of their own careerist interests. A few students were able to weave a web of contradictions. They cited how McNamara's demands for the "objective" eliminated the possibility of "soft" data, including the information futilely put forth by Ellsberg, and at the same time, contributed to corruption in "hard" data, including intentionally distorted reports of casualties, troop deployments, and enemy strength.

The details of this story illustrate a play within a play. These students, who were training to become industry's leaders, had made the "objective" responses they thought were required of them while studying a case illustrating the pitfalls of just such an approach.

After reading the second set of papers, the professor confronted them on their inconsistency. He handed back both papers and asked if they thought there was a difference. Without exception, the students acknowledged the superiority of the second effort.

The professor then asked, "Consider me the organization's spokesman. How could we have gotten your best and most candid effort on the first try?" The students replied,

"The answer is implicit in what just took place. Don't grade us." The professor challenged back, expressing the organization's dilemma, "You mean to tell me that you really would have put in the thorough up-front analysis that brought you to the point where you could print out with excellence, if you thought this paper wasn't going to be graded?!"

This challenge caused students to think. They reflected on the disorientation that befell them and the poor quality product delivered to their "organization" when they responded to the organizational request by suppressing the personal side of their reactions. They saw themselves like McNamara, vulnerable to having their "objective" responses decoded and used against them. And they saw themselves like the generals. They too were willing to say what they thought their boss (the professor) wanted to hear in the service of getting him to take action that furthered their personal interests—that is, their success in the course.

Above all, the students' experience illustrates a dilemma that plagues every organization: can the conditions for excellence be created without setting up systems of evaluation and reward that are disorienting to the people involved? Why couldn't at least one of twenty-five students tell it straight the first time? Let's pursue this question by considering a second example.

The consultant asked, "What's got you down today, Stu?" (Stu was a black personnel manager who, as a veteran of the 60's, had been there and back on civil rights.)

Stu replied, "Oh, it's this damn compliance guy who's ready to cite us for failure to live up to EEO (Equal Employment Opportunity) legislation. I'm breaking my back. Just once I'd like a letter saying I'm doing a good job."

"What's their problem?" asked the consultant.

Stu: "This time they're after me to hire Blacks and Chicanos into our professional and managerial ranks."

Consultant: "You may hate me for saying this, but I think they've got a good case. I haven't seen any minorities around here besides you."

"There aren't," Stu exclaimed, "I bring in two or three a week but I can't get my department managers to hire them. They say they're out to hire the best qualified person and that they're not going to compromise their department's performance just to get a minority in there. I tell them I'm bringing in the best talent on the job market and they tell me, 'You're doing a bang-up job, Stu, don't take it personally. There just aren't any good ones around!' "

Consultant: "So what are you going to do?"

Stu: "Keep the fashion show moving, I guess. What else can I do?" Then Stu leaned back in his chair and reflected, "I should have gone into business for myself when I had the chance. That's the only way to accomplish something you believe in."

The consultant jarred Stu by responding, "Just give me three months' notice before you do, then we'll insist on some real action!"

With that, Stu realized that he had been taken in by how his organization was allowing him to succeed. Here he was succeeding in the eyes of others while failing both himself and the organization. His managers called him a success because he was bringing candidates to their door but Stu's personal commitment to civil rights had been reduced to counting the number of people he brought in (form) rather than the number he was able to hire, train and then support (function). At the same time, his company's failure to live up to federal legislation was bringing it dangerously close to losing its government contracts. Yet, until the consultant took him to task,

Stu felt clean in his own mind. Again put in touch with his own inner commitment, he could risk doing what he thought was right. After a day of deliberation he decided to write the compliance officer agreeing that his company was not making any real progress and explaining why. He also sent copies to each of his managers. Six weeks later, Stu's company was well on its way toward compliance.

Now if you think the disparity between what people think the organization rewards and personal commitments confuse MBA students and people in business, you ought to see the disorientation of those working in the public sector. What the military calls "ticket punching" (getting points for doing the "right" thing—form—as contrasted with actually doing a good job—function) becomes absolutely crucial for survival.

———◆———

The consultant called it a "zoo." That was the only term he could come up with in offering words of empathy to the people he had just interviewed. He had been called in by the newly appointed director of a state agency with a $30 million a year budget to help in developing more effective management. He had merely been told that there were some problems.

Typical of his way of proceeding, the consultant began by interviewing the director and each of his deputies about their responsibilities and about what they thought was required to increase agency effectiveness. However, by midafternoon, he couldn't tolerate any more of what he was hearing, so he cancelled his remaining interviews, and sat quietly trying to figure out the meaning of what he had just learned.

In his ten years of management consulting, the consultant had never experienced a work group with such dramatically competitive views operating in such blatantly hostile ways. He heard about a deputy who had threatened to leak

information to the press that would greatly influence public opinion toward an upcoming voter referendum, if he
wasn't given assurances that he would not be fired after the
election. He heard about a deputy stealing a desirable office
at three in the morning and daring anyone to move him
out. He heard about a deputy who for weeks had successfully carried out the threat that her department would not
do any work until she received the additional personnel she
had requested.

It was relatively easy for the consultant to see the cause
of these difficulties, although he didn't know what to do
about them or even how to communicate them. In being
treated to seven very different descriptions of reality he was
disoriented which was also the organization's problem. Here
were the same players with the same organization mandate, experiencing the same events, but with each person
labeling things quite differently.

The consultant reflected on what forces could drive people to the infighting he had just heard reported. He saw a
condition endemic to the public sector caused by people
who want to care but who are too high up to get much protection out of civil service. In the upper levels of government, people, administrations, and job descriptions shift so
rapidly that no one can count on having a boss who's around
long enough to lend much protection. High-level civil ser-
vants, like these deputies, experience themselves as free
agents adrift in a bureaucracy, who would have perished
long ago had they not mastered the art of self-preservation.
Their futures have always depended on having something
tangible to show for each period of employment whether
or not what they produce makes much of a contribution to
the organization effort. The important thing is to produce
reports and other tangible monuments that one can point
to when looking for a new job or trying to establish oneself
with a new boss. The result is a careerist mentality—one

focuses on what the system rewards while smokescreening his or her limited involvement and cooperation in all other areas.

Given such divergent pictures of reality, what could the consultant report back to the group that would be heard the same way? That's how he hit upon the term "zoo"—at least everybody would recognize that he was talking about their situation. He told the group that he had not heard anyone offer a reason for why someone thought differently— that is, other than how the other person was "full of bull." He proposed that their best chance for civility and coordination would come from sharing career pictures with one another. A goal as lofty as collaboration would have to wait a while. He suggested that group members spend a day merely describing where they had been professionally and what they were trying to achieve personally in their government careers.

The consultant realized that his suggestion was a long way off from what he had been expected to do. He was hired to help individual deputies declare themselves against a mandated set of organization goals and to come to agreement on criteria for measuring their departments' performance. But he sensed that engaging this task directly would make him a co-conspirator in the careerist game. He could see no real improvement in the deputies' disorientation until they developed greater empathy for what the other person was trying to achieve. The consultant hoped such empathy would produce an appreciation for how these deputies could rely on one another in accomplishing projects that would give them a creditable image in the system. He hoped it would lead to candid group discussions in which organization needs for productivity could be discussed in the practical light of personal motivations and interests.

More than ever before, the consultant saw how each individual's need for success could subvert an organization from its mission. People always seem to find a way to succeed; organizations, particularly in the public sector, do not. As long as the director and his deputies could deny or put down the other person's career interests they produced the very infighting that reinforced careerist behavior. They became preoccupied with what the other person was personally out to achieve and could not hold constructive discussions about task.

---

At this point, we can't honestly continue without mentioning one of the most blatant examples where survival tactics subvert organizational excellence and where disoriented individuals succeed while the system wallows in mediocrity. This is found in our profession, university teaching. Actually, calling the profession "university teaching" is a misnomer. Despite speech after speech declaring the contrary, most professors get promoted on the basis of *how much they publish*. It's this way at UCLA, and it's this way at every ranking university of which we know.

Actually the people who evaluate professors—university administrators and other professors—are on to the disorientation and they attempt to consider the quality of what is published along with the quantity. They understand that the purpose of publishing goes beyond just creating knowledge. The purpose is to produce quality knowledge that is useful. But there are endless issues involved in evaluating quality within such a broad activity as "creating knowledge." Inevitably evaluators fall back to deliberating how much quantity compensates for what lack of quality, creativity and relevance. Such deliberations have become nearly a burlesque at a leading southern university where promotions have been put on a point system. Each step on the promotion ladder requires so many points. Four points are given for publishing in a top journal, two for a mediocre, more points for single-author articles, and so on.

Some of these professors are on editorial boards of journals, and they are thus encouraged to accept only those articles which support and value their own research. In our estimation, this university's system is the ultimate in encouraging careerism, not just among its own professors, but within entire disciplines of "scientific" inquiry.

To summarize, we have sought to present concrete illustrations of how the forms that signify success in the system can disorient individuals, work groups, and even entire organizations. We saw how students coping with the McNamara case were not able to write down what they truly valued until they were released from the form in which they thought their organization wanted their "excellence." We saw how a black personnel manager was able to succeed in the minds of his colleagues while not accomplishing what both he and the organization needed to achieve real success. Through the eyes of a management consultant, we saw how well-intentioned bureaucrats were easily forced into competitive, careerist, backstabbing antics where form replaced function. And we touched on what professors who might have liked to investigate what they personally valued were up against because of their desire to succeed in the system. In each instance, in the face of highly individualistic participation, the very performance standards that the organization set up to insure excellence wound up undermining it.

# 10 | REORIENTATION

The preceding chapter illustrates the ease with which people, organizations, and institutions become disoriented, either bogged down in internal strife or focused in directions that are at odds with their major opportunities and mission. In fact, the daily use of framing, fragmenting and playing-it-both-ways leads inevitably to disorientation—making it a natural and expected feature of organization life. Given the ease with which disorientation takes place, and the genuine desire of people to avoid the vicious infighting that accompanies disorientation, it is not surprising that efforts to realign stuck organizations spark a great deal of enthusiasm and support. However, in the absence of an understanding of the roots of disorientation, even the most sincere efforts to produce collaboration can go awry.

Now we'd like to take you through one of the most revealing experiments we've come upon in learning what else is needed to stem the tide of disorientation. It's an example of people energetically attempting to collaborate by subordinating self-interests to the needs of the organization and coming up short because common sense logic let them down. Follow along and see if you don't agree that most of the bases got covered and that the participants deserved results far better than the ones they received.

---

### The Experiment

This experiment took place in the engineering division of a large corporation.

Division top management had decided that it was now time to reorganize and make divisional operations more responsive to the needs of the business and to the people involved. More precisely, they were responding to pressures from V.P.s above, from middle managers, and from engineers at the very bottom. V.P.s were troubled that the division's organization chart did not fit well with the ones used by the manufacturing divisions that they were mandated to serve, and wanted changes that would provide a better fit and integration of engineering services. Middle managers were critical of the quality of the work being turned out by the division and were trying to place the blame on their top managers' unwillingness to pay top dollar and recruit higher level talent rather than accept responsibility themselves. Project engineers were complaining that they felt like second-class citizens because current modes of distributing work assignments did not provide them adequate opportunity to exercise choice and influence a project's direction.

The concept of an experiment—to get everybody involved in reorienting divisional operations—was worked out by the division manager, his three deputies and their two long-standing organization consultants as they discussed the problems their division faced. The details were worked out when these six met with middle level managers who themselves had ideas about the type of collaboration that would put divisional operations on firmer ground. Together they decided on the following, which, before it was actually implemented, was energetically affirmed by each level of their organization.

Each supervisor, from lowest level on up, was asked to meet with the people reporting to him or her to identify the other organizational units affecting the quality of their work. Once identified, the group would be asked to list the specific actions these other units took which helped or hindered their operations. Supervisors would then present what they learned at a huge feedback session, attended first by other supervisors, and later joined by the four upper level managers. The consultants were to be present at all sessions to facilitate open discussion and to help people with their analyses.

Everyone was told that the plan was expected to produce reorientation at three levels.

At the first level, the plan called for each person to systematically consider all influences bearing on his or her effectiveness, to then share these perceptions with work associates, to challenge others and to be challenged, and to initiate corrective action wherever possible.

At the second level, each supervisor would receive feedback on his or her own group's performance from every interfacing unit. Supervisors would also see the feedback given to each of the other units. They then would hold exchanges to clarify and deal with the problems other groups had with the way their units were conducting their operations. It was reasoned that reorientation requires people at every level ascertaining where their problems lie and actively involved in finding solutions in domains that they can influence.

*At the third level,* the four top managers would receive a thorough mapping of all the performance issues experienced by the personnel inside their division. Additionally they agreed to interview managers outside their division whose position gave them a slant on the engineering division's effectiveness. Of particular interest to them were managers from manufacturing divisions. Thus external as well as internal perspectives would be considered before making major changes.

In stating these expectations, managers tried to emphasize their belief that each person was dealing with a moving target and that, on a daily basis, people would be making decisions based on the new insights and perspectives they were receiving. Managers also promised to do their best not to fault individuals for specific problems uncovered.

This was to be an exercise in divisional improvement, not personnel evaluation.

### Enrichments

The experiment proceeded as expected, although a few enrichments were added.

At the meeting called to solicit supervisor support, a need was expressed to clarify and possibly restructure the steps a typical engineering project went through from start to completion. Accordingly, a task force representing various hierarchical levels and various project roles was formed to reconsider work flow and make recommendations. Another enrichment was added at the meeting called to discuss feedback. Representatives observed that enough overlap existed to identify a number of common themes underlying the concerns voiced by each of the groups. These were listed and used by the supervisors in their feedback sessions with subordinates. Incidentally, several of these themes were critical of division top management. In particular, people at all levels were suffering from the absence of performance evaluation. This was emphasized in some detail once the division manager and his three deputies joined the meeting. Specific remedies were proposed and agreed upon which made performance feedback a regularly occurring event.

After the feedback meeting with supervisors, upper-level managers and the consultants met to sort out what had been learned and to plan the reorganization. This produced some fiery exchanges and their analysis boiled down to three or four alternatives that would have to be tested with their bosses, the VPs. Sounding out their bosses brought agreement for one of these alternatives. The managers then set about interviewing candidates for the new jobs created by that alternative. Before finalizing their discussion and actually committing themselves to specific personnel, the managers went back to individual units to test those features of what was being proposed that would affect that unit and to talk personalities as well.

Perfect! To this point everything had gone more or less as desired.

## Conflict Erupts: The Experiment Ends in Failure

Three months after the initial feedback session, management called a meeting to publicly announce the revised organization chart with the accompanying changes in personnel. Suddenly conflict erupted; the meeting degenerated into a display of staff and lower-level manager furor. The cries went out: "Don't tell me this is all there is to your plan? I fail to see how it does anything for 12 of the 22 problems my group listed." "What's our guarantee that your adding two new departments is going to relieve the bottlenecks you tell us they will?" "Why didn't you include some of us in your deliberations?" Overall, the lower levels responded angrily saying that they felt their inputs had been ignored, that management was not doing enough to improve overall division effectiveness. To this the four managers responded defensively, and the consultants futilely attempted to retrace the history of their approach. The consultants tried to show how changes on the organization chart represented only a small part of the total effort marshalled to improve the organization's effectiveness. Most of the improvement was supposed to come from widespread understanding of the overall situation—enabling people at every level to solve problems within their own jurisdiction.

Nothing could untangle the confusion. Statements made by lower-level employees revealed their belief that a "collaborative" effort required nothing more from them than listing what was and continued to be wrong. They forgot how they had been asked to confront their role in it. Statements made by the top managers revealed little more than dismay that people in the lower ranks could not appreciate the roles they played and must continue to play in improving the effectiveness of the division. As the discussion went on, what little clarity there was deteriorated further. The engineers reverted back to reciting their laundry list of criticisms, dumping them out without offering much in the way of helping with solutions. In response the top managers behaved paternalistically by listening courteously to these complaints and appearing to take all the responsibility for making things right.

Everyone had bailed out.

------

## *What Went Wrong?*

Given the times it's hard to find much fault with how this well-intentioned cast tried to proceed. However our theory shows us what should have been done differently.

For one thing, three months was probably too long for people to go without "scoring" on the traditional organization checklist, wondering whether their self-critique and collaborative efforts would pay off. No doubt everyone felt naked and overexposed when the others decided to run for cover. Consider what was involved.

Employees at the middle and lower levels were required to place themselves in the awkward position of saying essentially, "I'm going to do everything possible to expose my problems and personal faults and make an all out effort to correct them." Such a position makes people vulnerable to upper-level criticism and ensures that they will be found lacking. On the other hand, refusing to confess or to be open in the face of other people's criticisms creates the impression that one is not willing to go all out for the "good" of the organization. No wonder those at the lower levels retreated with a case of instant amnesia.

Upper-level managers were also placed in an awkward position. They found themselves being challenged to publicly demonstrate an openness to all suggestions and to share all their data, including what they learned from corporate higher-ups—data someone at a lower level would need in formulating a viable alternative. Doing either would again make them vulnerable. They couldn't allow other corporate managers to see them abandoning their decision-making powers and they did not want subordinates to have the data that possibly could show up their alternative as suboptimal. On the other hand, they couldn't admit this for fear of giving the impression that they did not value employee initiative, inputs, and involvement that went beyond the scope of formal job responsibilities. No wonder they jumped at the opportunity to seize the controls.

Life is seldom as intentional as our analysis would have it. It is almost impossible to separate after-the-fact justifications from before-the-fact intentions. By the time the new plan was announced, employees actually believed they were being "had" and accepted little responsibility for the reorientation effort. To this day, the boss and his top managers contend that they did not *want* to seize controls, but neither could they afford to leave the impression that the division was faltering for a lack of decisive leadership.

## Can Collaboration Work?

Is it possible for people to put self-interests aside in working for the greater organization good? Is it possible to establish the criteria for each person's success so that everyone in a hierarchical chain benefits from the organization's effectiveness? These questions should produce humility in light of what we've just seen. An all-out effort to put self-interests aside, optimal circumstances, and the participants still couldn't pull it off.

Why couldn't they pull it off? We believe it's because the participants lacked a concept like alignment to alert them to all that the experiment was asking them to do. They thought they were merely being asked to suspend the expression of some self-interests which they were only too happy to do. The concept of alignment, though, shows us that much more was involved. The experiment was asking people to suspend their internal orientations and they didn't know how to relate to their work without them.

---

## Alignments

Recall that alignments are the basic guidance systems that tell people how to navigate through organizational happenings that have little intrinsic meaning outside of that which people are assigning to them. Alignments tell people how to do their job, how to interpret each organization event, and how to responsibly fulfill their organizational duties without neglecting the personal reasons which brought them to their job in the first place. People lose sight of the purpose behind sacrificing for the greater organization good when their alignment is suspended. Organizational collaboration becomes impossible because the people involved are disoriented.

In our judgment, this experiment was conceived in the alignment of top management and carried out at the expense of lower downs. It is top management who is charged with improving overall organization effectiveness and they have the most to gain when their organization is operating effectively and is perceived that way. Their job is coordination, planning, and integration. Getting subordinates to accept more responsibility for these functions insures their effectiveness. But middle managers who nondefensively open themselves to all problems in their work unit's effectiveness and at the same time sign on for the thankless role of making other units more aware of theirs, expand their responsibilities while adding to their vulnerability. Likewise, project engineers who concern themselves with lofty issues of coordination and integration while their evaluation depends primarily on the quality of their own technical output do themselves a disservice. To play the organization game differently, lower downs would need new formal mandates—ones that paid off for their new endeavors while offering protection against the vulnerability they incur for not scoring in traditional ways. To the best of our knowledge, no discussions were held about new leniencies in current responsibilities or the pay-offs for expanded ones.

The experiment also presented a few alignment dilemmas for top management. Creating a forum in which organization functions and roles are critiqued is not particularly threatening as long as the top managers are not called upon to produce the data, inputs, and compromises on which their decisions are based. After all, upper levels can always derive protection from the well-accepted organization logic that goes, "If you knew what I knew but can't divulge and were facing the pressures I was under, you probably would have done the same." Logic like this serves an important purpose in most organizations since the higher one goes, the more ambiguity one faces and the greater the number of subjectively based decisions and arbitrary judgments one makes. It's top management who decides which goals the organization addresses, which benchmarks denote progress, which formal roles need to be performed, and so forth. Accordingly, it's the top management that has the most territory to defend, the most personal latitudes to protect and the greatest number of personal indulgences to hide. In this instance, top managers retreated behind closed doors to hammer out their differences and compose a new organization chart. How else could they protect themselves from those Monday morning quarterbacks with their own personal investments.

---

Our analysis leaves us concluding that real collaboration was not possible because people lacked constructs like the one we call alignment which might have provided a beginning to

their appreciating the unique dilemmas they and others encountered in orienting to organization events. But in today's
organizational world, a concept such as alignment introduces
a note of subjectivity that is equated with personal indulgence
and organizational ineffectiveness. So the fight picked up over
what each group genuinely felt were promised expectations.
Each group felt betrayed seeing the other group not delivering on their promises and they were unable to hold the conversation that would allow group members to see what was
fundamentally amiss.

# 11 | ALIGNMENT
IS THE KEY

By now we hope readers appreciate that understanding people's alignments is the key to understanding what organizations are really about. Only when you're aware of self-interests
can you detect that many "objective" assessments of problems, goals, or facts represent arbitrary and self-convenient
constructions of reality made by people who are trying to find
personally meaningful ways to do their jobs. Admittedly, even
without reading this book, most people agree this is true. But
when we examine their daily actions, we find few people
showing respect for what is arbitrary and self-convenient in
the conduct of organization tasks. People operate with imperatives and absolutes as if the problems they are pursuing,

the goals they are addressing, and the facts they are portraying were revealed to them behind the burning bush.

---

To us the actions of the recently retired Police Chief of Los Angeles, Chief Ed Davis, exemplify most people's behavior. The Chief had two skills but not a third which, with his personality, led him to some bizarre organizational exchanges. First the Chief was skilled in framing reality in ways which were convincingly tailored to his unique alignment. Next he was skilled in spotting when others were presenting a reality that posed problems for his alignment and in penetrating their "factual" representations of the truth to display that which was arbitrary and self-serving. But the Chief was *not* at all skilled in recognizing the arbitrary and self-convenient biases in his own presentations and the fact that his orientation was every bit as subjective as those of the people he took to task.

For this reason, watching the Chief provides a learning opportunity for all of us. His double standard thinking led him to attack his critics for their self-serving behavior with the indignation of someone whose own portrayal of the facts was nothing less than objective. For example, look at how the Chief operated when he spotted self-interests in the *Los Angeles Times** "objective" portrayal of the news, and the way he decided to take this newspaper on.

In a letter published on the editorial page of the *Times*, Chief Davis stated why he had no choice but to cancel the Davis family's subscription to the *Times*, a subscription that had begun in 1890. The Chief was upset because of the blatant ways *Times* reporters colored the news. On the

* August 20, 1975.

social front he believed the paper had developed into an organ of "moral revisionism," conditioning its readers to a new set of values which condoned homosexuality and marijuana. On the personal front he cited the *Times'* "1975 war on me in which . . . almost every reporter who has any part in reporting anything I have said has engaged in repeated slanted reporting and downright lies." The Chief said, "If it wasn't so consistent, I could understand and excuse occasional mistakes. You (The *Times*) are the masters of selective reporting, impressionistic journalism, direct misquotes—even to the point of omitting portions within quotes without notifying the reader. All of this adds up to, in effect, being a journalistic liar." The Chief concluded his protest by saying he was discontinuing his subscription because ". . . I am afraid I might believe something that you have written which is the reverse of the truth, and when it's in an area beyond my ability to perceive, I am liable to believe it and, therefore, will be poisoning my mind with misinformation."

On the surface, we see a ridiculous situation. We find the Chief of Police of Los Angeles asserting that no longer is he going to read the only major newspaper in the whole of Southern California. But it took only two weeks for the Chief to be caught referring to a current *Times* article. Confronted by a reporter, the Chief laughed off the inconsistency, saying that top aides have found ways to slip him articles he ought to see, but in a form that's not likely to contaminate his viewpoint.

Putting aside the comic aspects, we can see the Chief identifying self-interests in the *Times'* presentation of the news, but not acknowledging them in his own actions. The Chief's sensitivity to the self-interests which influence what reporters and editorial news writers publish is particularly sharp because their slanting of the news is so contrary to his point of view.

A long-standing critic of social deviants, judicial permissiveness, pornography, grass, and prostitution, he realizes that his views and advocacy are in danger once he starts viewing the world in the categories used by the *Times'* staff. He understands that value-laden reporting takes place not only on the editorial pages but throughout the paper and that as a result he is being forced to differentiate self-serving realities from what is labeled an "objective" portrayal of the news. The Chief fears having the *Times'* orientation covertly substituted for his own.

We have a great deal of empathy with the Chief's concern, although we don't share his law-and-order politics. The Chief is fearful of an orientation that is being portrayed as objective, while it's actually subjective and thus variable. However, he responded with a subjective response of his own—invoking a double standard. In labeling the *Times'* staff "journalistic liars," he implied that there is only one correct way to tell a story, that his orientation was the given, and that the *Times* was guilty of deceit. He came on as if he was never guilty of trying to impose his categories on others. But the Chief was noted for his parochial viewpoint. His politics and conservative social stance had long served as a rallying point for tough-minded law-and-order advocates. Certainly no one would suspect him of writing a letter to the doctrinaire *Police Gazette* complaining that it was subverting his viewpoint.

Chief Davis became indignant that the *Times'* commitment to selling newspapers was stronger than its commitment to portraying him in a flattering light. Once the Chief saw through the *Times'* "objectivity" he knew exactly what to do— denounce the *Times* for its subjectivity. From one perspective this was a smart tactic for him to employ. From another, it displayed a naivete that's characteristic of us all. *There is absolutely no reason to expect others to approach organizational happenings with a reality that mirrors our own.* This is the most basic and overlooked fact of organization life. People possess unique alignments that cause them to view events primarily in terms of what they mean to them personally.

At this point we'd like the reader to come to a screeching halt because we're set up to counter an assumption of the Chief's which most people also make but which distorts their views of organization life. It's a self-deception that finds people talking as if they understand alignment, that is, that they understand that everyone views work events with a unique perspective, while faulting others, like the Chief did, when they fail to demonstrate "objectivity" by failing to see things in a *particular* way. It has people believing that others approach them with highly individualistic and variable orientations while living, as the Chief did, as if there is one objective orientation which must be sought and implemented. In short, people talk as if they have an appreciation for how each individual's success depends on pursuing a unique orientation to reality but their actions and treatment of those who differ with them do not reflect such an appreciation.

This is an important finding because, simple as it sounds, the organization world looks and feels quite differently once someone actually develops an internalized grasp of alignment and pursues his or her organizational course with the uniqueness of people's commitments in mind. In fact, consider the following differences and see if you don't agree that they make perfect sense in terms of the issues we've been discussing in this book, although they deviate sharply from how most people think and conduct their everyday affairs.

FIRST — *Self-interests are operating all the time and there is nothing necessarily sinister about their presence.*

Thinking this does not mean abandoning organizations to the self-serving whims of people. Instead it means acknowledging that self-interests are already part of the everyday fabric of organization events and that one's time is better spent appreciating others' unique directions than finding fault with their less than objective orientations to their jobs. If Chief Davis' letter shows one thing clearly, it shows the power that someone with a competing viewpoint can exert in uncovering biases that go unnoticed by more compatible viewpoints. The Chief spotted the *Times'* less than objective orientation with laser-like accuracy. Unfortunately, the Chief's personal involvement served to discredit him as a fair minded critic.

> SECOND — *Alignment helps us see that there is an equifinality to most organizational actions—that is, there are many routes from A to B with valuable organization payoffs associated with each of them.*

Failure to realize this leads people to out-of-hand reject proposals that do not line up well with their own and to miss the bona fide missions these proposals were formulated to advance. Chief Davis made a futile attempt to dismiss the *Times* as if spotting their bias gave him just cause for overlooking the many ways in which *Times'* reporters support police department work. The idea is to discriminate between instances in which someone's unique self-expression and inevitable bias come at the actual expense of organization effectiveness, and instances in which someone's unique stance merely makes it tougher for us to successfully pursue our own interests.

> THIRD — *Alignment helps us see the inadequacies contained in accepted procedures for conducting evaluation and the futility of holding others accountable without first having an in-depth understanding of the unique directions they are attempting to pursue.*

People who get evaluated without consideration for their alignment are likely to find some of their best contributions faulted for not measuring up to performance standards that they never set out to accomplish. Reciprocally, if there is one thing that characterizes organizations today, it is a group of disappointed evaluators after-the-fact sitting around trying to figure out why people failed to perform well on standards that they thought were clear from the first. We believe that Chief Davis would make his point more effectively by articulating the alignment issues distinguishing his department's activities from the evaluation system used by the *Times* instead of getting caught up claiming "foul," preoccupied with the injustices being done to him. Valid approaches to evaluation and accountability are two-way processes in which evaluator and evaluatee alike declare their preferred orientations and in advance figure out where their interests are likely to be incompatible.

FOURTH — *Alignment helps us see the highly politicized underpinnings of everyday organization life.*

Successful pursuit of self-interests depends on the meanings which get attached to one's activities. This is not to say that people get by with low competence or with minimal organizational contribution, but it is to say that vested interests are ever present. All acts that individuals perform and all evaluations they make are postured in their alignment. Posturing and image building are at least as important as the intrinsic value of the service rendered or product produced. Chief Davis knew this. He understood that his department's reputation and success hinged on such points as whether *Times* readers bought the thinking that police energy was being wasted in cracking down on "victimless" crimes such as pot smoking and prostitution. The same issue is present for all of us. A boss must fight to the death to get himself labeled as a "far-ranging manager who does a great job handling a department as technical as manufacturing" while disappointed subordinates angle for a label that implies that he is "a manufacturing manager who lacks the technical expertise to give us adequate direction." There is no one objective way to have one's performance viewed and alignment explains the underlying dynamics and what's at stake.

FIFTH — *Alignment helps us appreciate the variability and impermanence of what on any given day gets portrayed as the bottom line.*

What constitutes finished product, financial solvency, the organization's mission, or even hard earnings cannot be viewed independently of what people set out to accomplish, and the criteria that best serve their interests. Instinctively, Chief Davis detected that something was off with the standards the *Times* was using to measure his department's performance and he was rowing against the tide trying to change this. Like Chief Davis, all people must learn how to go beyond the practice of hauling out so-called bottom-line criteria which are chosen for self-convenience as much as anything else. In today's organizations the dangers of treating high scores on a particular set of indices as if they are sufficient to establish that the organization is operating effectively, with no further explanations necessary, are becoming increasingly apparent. Certainly there will be new criteria tomorrow, because even today we are seeing problems with such "absolute" measures as net income, earnings per share, numbers of minorities employed, and so forth. Those who observe an overcommitment to yesterday's benchmarks and who are not open-minded to the emergence of new standards are highly vulnerable to personal and professional obsolescence.

---

Is this way of operating inevitable? What if the conversations could be held—conversations in which the centrality of personal alignments were an accepted fact of organization life, conversations in which people could openly acknowledge the foolhardiness involved in setting up controls to get rid of self-interests, and conversations in which people could actively search for better ways to line up self-interests with organizational pursuits. Then how would organizations look?

# TRULY OBJECTIVE MANAGEMENT

IV

Thus far we have shown that what is currently called "objective" in management is in reality highly subjective and that the justifications people give for their actions vary from the actual reasoning they use. Now we can show you how to produce *truly* objective management by connecting managerial actions with their actual motivations. We're ready to transform our appreciation for the deeply rooted way self-interests operate into practical recommendations aimed at permitting you to succeed without adding to the existing chaos.

In constructing our recommendations, we first asked ourselves, "Where within the existing processes of organization can our readers reap the most immediate and direct benefits of our theory?" The answer was obvious. We can give you considerable help with the difficult and sensitive areas of evaluation and accountability. Accordingly, in Chapters 12 and 13 we explain how you can unilaterally influence the processes of evaluation and accountability in ways we believe will benefit both yourself and your organization.

In the final three chapters we describe the longer term and more comprehensive developments our theory suggests. Overall, we see organizations changing markedly under the impetus of a critical mass of people who understand how alignments are formed and how alignments determine reactions to organization happenings. Chapter 14 describes an educational process that creates this perspective. Chapters 15 and 16 present what we believe are new and original outlooks on the type of power that accrues from having this perspective and the kind of leadership necessary to foster it. Each chapter comes with specific pointers which we hope will help you to acquire the skills necessary for putting this understanding into action.

# 12 | A NEW LOOK AT EVALUATION

Now we're ready to attack evaluation head on and to appreciate why it has become the scourge of organization life. As practiced today, evaluation is the activity in which all the problems created by the war of meanings converge. It's during evaluations that people express their implicit and idiosyncratic needs as absolute judgments and seek to find out why others have not performed as expected. Since nowhere along the line have these expectations been voiced, more often than not the evaluatees find themselves under fire for failing to meet standards they never knew existed.

The concept of alignment lets us understand that there is no performance that can please all evaluators' self-beneficial orientations. Recognizing this paves the way for some practical pointers which, at a minimum, increases one's chances of making it through the type of "objectivity" that gets applied during evaluations.

> POINTER #1 — *No matter how peaceful the setting, keep in mind that you are being evaluated every minute of every day.*

Don't let yourself think you can succeed merely by doing what's "right" and letting the chips fall where they may. Since you are under constant scrutiny by everyone whose alignment is affected by the way you do your job, a war of meaning is taking place, even if the action isn't visible. Those around you are poised to attack. All they need is a cue that the meanings, commitments, and outcomes that are important to you are at odds with what they want to see accomplished.

> POINTER #2 — *There is one exception to the above. The one time when you are not being evaluated is when someone blows the whistle and calls "time" for your evaluation.*

At that moment it's the evaluators who are being evaluated, not you. They've already drawn their conclusions, now they must convince you and justify their position to the wider organization. And, even more importantly to them, they've got to project an image of "objectivity." They'll settle for the "right" point with the wrong specifics. They're likely to cite anything that gives credibility to the conclusions they have already drawn.

> POINTER #3 — *Make every effort to comprehend the alignment of your evaluators before you let them sit you down for a performance review.*

(Moreover, if you can pull it off, get your evaluator to state his or her orientation out loud.) Evaluators have a way of sounding absolute. They frequently come on as if they have the precise slant you lack and must acquire in order to be viewed as competent. But they have alignments just as you do. Keep in mind that it's always a struggle to maintain a sense of your personal priorities, and now you must additionally contend with evaluators who come on as if they have the very perspective you need to succeed. Maintaining your own directions while open-mindedly listening to them requires an understanding of your evaluators' orientations and, better yet, some of the personal reasons behind them.

POINTER #4 — *Do your best not to allow formal evaluation to take place before your evaluators truly understand the unique vantage point from which your talents and contributions look strongest.*

During evaluation two issues readily get confused. The first concerns your alignment and what constitutes personal success for you. The second has to do with how the contributions generated by your alignment fit with the alignments of others in the organization. In the heat of evaluation, the first easily gets confused with the second. Evaluators operate as if you are striving to achieve what they want you to achieve with the evaluation session producing an expression of how adequate you are, not how good a fit exists, or could exist, between you and the organization. In the end, you can feel abused while your evaluator feels guilty. He or she has had to prove that you were inadequate when it was only necessary to demonstrate a poor fit.

POINTER #5 — *Don't let your evaluators disconnect your activities from the goals you are striving to attain.*

On a daily basis, few people actually achieve major accomplishments—they merely make a little progress toward their goals. But evaluation is a moment by moment event, and others need a "roadmap" to value what they see you doing. They are dependent on you for this orientation. When you don't give it, they're likely to sit around thinking about what you ought to be doing, which usually you're not because what occurs spontaneously to others seldom makes much sense from your way of seeing things. In fact, the sure-fire signal that an evaluator lacks such an orientation is an assignment which you experience as a "fire drill" or "exercise." Usually such assignments make perfect sense in your evaluator's structure and are made because your evaluator wants to sleep nights and can't until he or she sees you engaging in the activities in which he or she would engage if pursuing the goals to which it was thought you had agreed.

> POINTER #6 — *Don't let your evaluators disconnect themselves from their responsibility for creating the conditions that allow you to succeed.*

Many evaluators have a way of agreeing with others' objectives but conducting themselves in ways which undermine their means. Moreover, most supervisors are absolutely ingenious at finding ways to walk away from their subordinates' failures without damaging their own prestige. They do this by denying responsibility for their role in establishing the unique conditions necessary for a particular approach to a problem. It's up to you, and no one else, to make sure that evaluators comprehend the conditions that are favorable to what you are trying to achieve and that they receive feedback when their actions make life difficult for you.

> POINTER #7 — *At the "evaluation session," don't waste too much energy arguing with your evaluator.*

At that point, arguing seldom gets you anywhere; you're better off using the time to figure out where the evaluators are coming from and if you don't agree tell them that you don't. Tell them you see the events differently but don't argue details. Arguing merely risks adding to what your evaluators see as wrong. If you do, you've got all the problems your evaluator just listed plus you're "defensive." No one expects you to be perfect, but defensiveness is a characteristic that your detractors can latch onto later on when you set out to show that they lacked a valid perspective for viewing your contribution or when you contritely decide to make a case for "rehabilitation."

POINTER #8 — *Don't get lulled to sleep by a globally positive evaluation.*

Unqualified praise is a setup. The only thing it means for certain is that you are operating in a way that fits someone's convenience. It may also mean that you are doing a good job. But that will be only because you are sufficiently low in the organization to have limited responsibilities and low visibility. The higher you make it in the hierarchy and/or the more central role you play in the organization's functioning, the more likely you are to see the world in ways that others will find necessary to criticize. In fact, interpersonally, a totally positive evaluation leads to pacts and expectations of reciprocity; personally, it creates insularity and attenuates growth; and organizationally, it leads to unrealistically high expectations for subsequent performances.

POINTER #9 — *Don't think that you can, on your own, adequately conceptualize the alignment or vantage point that best articulates the strength of your contributions.*

No one can. Everyone takes their situation too personally and possesses self-doubts from childhood which play right into their evaluator's criticisms. It's too easy to be intimidated by someone else's version of what the system absolutely requires to function effectively. Figuring out your strengths and the qualities you have to contribute requires the help of capable friends who understand your talents and personal priorities and who are behind your expression of what is unique in and essential to your makeup.

> POINTER #10 — *Be sure to maintain a vigil for those who are tracking you with an unsympathetic frame of reference.*

Nobody is perfect, nobody's bucket of talents and capacities to contribute is completely full. Nevertheless, some people will give you the benefit of the doubt, the generous interpretation, and some people will give you the opposite. You can tell your friends from your antagonists by how someone structures his or her feedback to you. Be alert for those who criticize what, in your frame of reference, feels like the fine points, while neglecting the major contributions. At least temporarily, their alignment is out of sync with yours and until you identify the differences, everything you say and do is likely to feed their criticisms of you.

> POINTER #11 — *Keep in mind that there's a time to fight and a time to walk, and try to avoid situations that force you to fight when you should be taking a walk.*

Fight for a more accurate evaluation when you believe an honest portrayal of your commitments has an opportunity of being viewed from an appreciative perspective. Walk, get out, once it becomes clear that evaluators must relate to you in a way that makes your accomplishments and strengths look weak or when the price of having evaluators see your strengths entails getting them to see too many of their own deficiencies.

Pointers such as these make it much easier to cope with the self-interest side of "objective" evaluation. They allow you to contrast what it takes to produce *personal success* with what it takes to receive a *positive evaluation*. Success depends on your own subjective standards. Personal success entails formulating an alignment that is responsive to self and organizational interests alike and pursuing that alignment in a self-satisfying way. On the other hand, positive evaluation depends on making it in someone else's subjective frame of reference. Others monitor what you do and stand for against the framework of their own highly personal orientations, albeit, that like you, their orientations encompass contributions to the organization.

Such pointers also underscore the importance of remaining conscious of the fact that evaluation is a moment by moment process in which each evaluatee has a major role to play. Each person must establish the unique images that make his or her commitments understood and valued and the conditions that make his or her contributions visible. And it's not enough to get credit merely for the outcomes you produce— you also need credit for participating in activities that produce outcomes. For instance we know an R & D department where only a single new product is produced each year, where far more effort goes into maintaining the department than is visible in that year's product, and where the manager who heads the department used to be under fire. Evaluators were critical of this manager and seemed to sit around wondering what he was up to on the 364 days a year when no breakthroughs were taking place. They simply lacked a roadmap for appreciating his daily involvements in priority setting, resource deployment, technical analysis, team building, and any number of other activities essential to producing innovation. When they got it, he got his credit. Today he's a success doing more or less what he always did.

## Evaluation and Organization Effectiveness

Thus far in the chapter we have focused on evaluation as if our theory applies only to those individuals who are in the process of being evaluated. However, our theory applies more broadly. In addition it alerts us to a series of evaluation issues which are not commonly viewed as such and which bear on organization effectiveness. To illustrate how our insights apply to everyday issues of organizational effectiveness, we are going to tell you about what has to be the toughest challenge we've run across in testing the practical applications of our perspective. It's a situation that boggles the mind of the organization viewer who does not appreciate the way alignments create an omnipresent air of evaluation. To the uninitiated it looked like an impossible situation. To us it represented an extreme example of someone experiencing competing demands from different evaluators and who felt too vulnerable to hold his evaluators accountable.

The featured player is Hank, the executive director of a goodsize state agency with about a $30 million a year budget.

At 35 Hank is an experienced bureaucrat whose smarts and dedication are never questioned. He is bright, exceptionally articulate, and thinks with systems logic. If he has any shortcomings, they lie in his strong desire to portray a "can-do" image. This leads him to make decisions for managers who hesitate and to set such an intense personal pace that even run-of-the-mill projects can sometimes take on an air of crisis.

On one hand Hank is responsible for a staff of 500, of which 350 are skilled professionals with little management experience. On the other, Hank is accountable to five full-time commissioners who literally are programmed not to agree. Each was appointed by the state's governor, to a five-year staggered term, to represent a specific point of view. In formal terms, commissioners decide agency policy while Hank's staff analyzes, implements and regulates. In practical terms, the outcomes of the staff's analysis and the character of their implementation impacts on the type of policy commissioners can support so that indirectly what the staff does influences what the commissioners can propose as public policy. The staff's influence is well appreciated by the five commissioners who, without the slightest hesitation, use strong-arm tactics in attempting to get staff to record their findings in ways that agree with the position the commissioner is programmed to take.

The impossibility of Hank's situation stems from his weak mandate and the ease with which he can be terminated. On any given day three commissioners can get together and vote him a dismissal. What's more, not one of the commissioners owes him a thing. The executive director's job had been vacant a while, and Hank was the "temporary" replacement who out-lasted the search committee. Consequently he never had the opportunity to extract the type of commitment that would allow him to operate with clout.

The governor designates one of the commissioners to be commission chairman and that person is supposed to serve as Hank's link to the other commissioners. Hank views the current chairman as an "administrative disaster" whose involvement in the formulation of public policy leads him to neglect practical matters of coordination and communication. Nevertheless Hank respects the chairman's social philosophy and thus feels loyal. In fact, Hank does his best to fill in the gaps, particularly in bringing the other commissioners up to speed with the chairman's thinking. Unfortunately, the commissioners cite Hank's involvement as evidence that he and the chairman are in cahoots. But this is a ploy aimed at his intimidation. Being accused of collusion causes Hank to defend himself by reassuring the challenging commissioner that he intends to fairly represent all points of view. In turn the commissioner uses Hank's reassurance as an opening to push his own views while attacking those of the other commissioners. In this way Hank and his top aides are treated to a continual stream of commissioner pressure in which the punch line is, "I'm OK. Keep in mind that the other commissioners are not. And you may be OK, that is—if you handle this one my way."

After about a year of struggling with this situation Hank sought the help of a consultant. Hank told him, "We've got to do something about the morale problems caused by the ways commissioners harass me and my senior staff and the feeling that I am not doing a sufficiently forceful job of protecting staff integrity." In particular, he was told about a crisis created by two commissioners who wanted a middle manager fired despite Hank's assertions that this manager was doing his job well. Everyone on the commission's staff knew these commissioners were trying to get the third vote necessary to override Hank. They also knew that Hank was dug in, ready to resign if he lost this one.

Studying the legislation that created the commission helped the consultant see the external forces underlying Hank's situation. By law, commissioners were appointed to represent divergent interests. This served as a check against the agency taking on a singular point of view. What's more, the chairman was one of the people who ran the governor's election campaign, and informally had the job of keeping the commission from causing trouble for the administration. Overall this structure ensured debate and the airing of wide-ranging perspectives—but competition among commissioners with different alignments created havoc.

Interviews with senior staff helped the consultant appreciate the internal forces at work. Faced with commissioners who must champion divergent interests, individuals on the staff saw no recourse but to play-it-both-ways. Their standard defense was to portray their perspectives with a vagueness which allowed them to appear on track to many viewpoints at once. This type of fragmentation protected them from commissioners but apparently at the cost of disorienting themselves. Top-level managers and staff could not, on demand, produce statements that connected their activities to what individual commissioners saw as the agency's priorities.

We'll spare you the rest of the details and take you directly to the session in which the consultant presented five recommendations to a group composed of Hank and his top management team. It displays the logic of our pointers on evaluation.

*First,* "Let's begin," the consultant said, "by recognizing that the commissioners have an impossible situation, too. Take a hard look at it sociologically before you get involved in personalities." He pointed out that the commissioners were young men with other journeys ahead. "Not only are they concerned with doing the best job for the state but each one needs the individual credit that will produce his next job or public appointment."

*Second,* the consultant advised, "Stop playing-it-both-ways. Why not declare yourselves as openly as possible and let the commissioners fight it out with one another? Make them decide whether your efforts should be redirected rather than trying to manipulate them covertly. If their stand doesn't make sense, then say so in your staff report and make it part of the public record."

*Third,* he said, "Once you've got sufficient agreement to move forward, tell the commissioners how you expect them to participate in supporting the overall agency effort. Let them hold you accountable for a quality analysis, but dammit, you hold them accountable for creating the conditions that allow you to produce one." As an example the consultant took up the problem of two commissioners pressuring to have a middle manager replaced. Turning to Hank, he asked, "Do you think they'd be calling for a vote on an individual personnel decision if you were publicly holding them accountable for how such a stand affects morale?"

*Fourth*, the consultant admonished the group for being unwitting foils in the commissioners' fights. "Don't let commissioners get away with putting one another down. When it happens, say something like, 'You know, when I was last with him and he put you down, I stuck up for you. Now I feel that you may be similarly in error.' "

*Fifth*, the consultant told Hank, "I think you should tell the commissioners that you are working closely with the Chairman, but specify that you are in 'cahoots' only on administrative issues and don't intend to interfere in policy." He continued, "In their minds, you're already guilty; you might just as well help them understand how."

This consultant was well versed in our theory and it's instructive to examine the understanding of organization dynamics on which his recommendations were based.

———◆———

*The first recommendation* reflects little more than an acknowledgment that *alignments* direct an individual's orientation and that when you see five people who you know are competent acting incompetently, you must search further than personalities to determine the cause. In this case the consultant urged agency staff to stop viewing the commissioners as insensitive evaluators and to start appreciating that their actions were better explained by the fact that they too were being evaluated by a diverse set of competing interests.

*The second recommendation* reflects the consultant's understanding of the evaluation conditions that force people to *fragment*. People play-it-both-ways when experiencing competing demands from constituencies who don't seem to give a damn about anything other than their own concerns. In this case, by not declaring themselves, the staff assumed the burden of the commissioners' disagreements and were aiding and abetting a process of bullying and nonconstructive debate.

*The third recommendation* embodies a much overlooked issue in evaluation. Both the evaluator and evaluatee must hold the other accountable. The consultant understands that it's never in the organization's interest to have evaluators running around without being accountable to the people they evaluate. When this happens, valid perspectives are overpowered and conformity flourishes. We'll have much more to say about this in the next chapter.

*The fourth recommendation* builds on the consultant's recognition that staff, like children with fighting parents, have a lot to gain by promoting rapport among their "elders." That the commissioners are going to disagree is built into their mandate, but their chances of finding a middle ground and making the best decision for the people of the state are greatly increased if they are encouraged to dignify their relationships by showing respect for the other's right to hold a differing point of view.

*The fifth recommendation* might have been the consultant's most important. He understood that everyone knew that self-interests play a big role in determining an organization's direction and that distrust flourishes when one person can't figure out the self-beneficial aspects for which a second is pushing. Denying the role his "partisan" interests play in improving the quality of commissioner interaction was the most crippling course that Hank could take. Therefore, the consultant merely asked Hank to be up front with his personal involvements and meet the commissioners head on.

Overall, the consultant showed Hank and his top managers

that their daily style of interaction left the commissioners with no valid data on which to base their evaluation of staff efforts, other than how well staff supported their own divergent special interest commitments, and that the key to successful evaluation lay in the informal use of routine day-to-day exchanges, not in semi-annual confrontations.

---

### Reflection

In this chapter we have been intent upon providing advice designed to enhance the reader's skills in the arena of performance evaluation—an arena in which the war of meanings is either present or on the horizon. In every instance our counsel is rooted in an understanding of the role alignments play in determining an evaluation. Armed with this understanding, we can appreciate:

- That when our efforts and activities are evaluated against commitments which represent our evaluators' alignments we, more often than not, will appear inefficient, indecisive and lacking in focus and coherence; and,

- That when our efforts and activities are evaluated against commitments which represent our own alignments we, more often than not, will appear effective, poised, highly integrated and spontaneous in our actions; and,

- That, other things being equal, we are more likely to have our efforts and activities evaluated against our evaluator's commitments than our own.

We are not cynical regarding this fundamental bias within evaluation. We view it as the inevitable consequence of a busy, complex and competitive organization world in which self-interests can only be discussed when there is an organizationally legitimate reason for being in competition. Hence formal evaluation puts one on the defensive and creates the need for pointers to minimize one's vulnerability, and a revised style of daily interaction offers the only chance to have one's actions appreciated in terms of the commitments which give rise to them.

# 13 | A NEW LOOK AT ACCOUNTABILITY

Now that we've given you some pointers on how to better your performance as an evaluatee, we're ready to move to the other side of the table. In this chapter, we show you how to produce real accountability, and how to objectively evaluate the performance of those who are working for you.

———————◆———————

Once again, your first step must be to recognize that subjective forces underlie "objective" standards of accountability. Thus, any valid attempt to produce truly objective accountability entails viewing what someone else is up to against the backdrop of *their* commitments, not your own. This means departing from how we conventionally reason whereby we assess other people's accomplishments in the context of our own orientation. Such conventional reasoning produces traps of the ilk some friends of ours fell into when sizing up the Japanese culture. They imputed caring and sensitivity to the stranger who graciously spent an hour helping them find their Tokyo Station train in the midst of the rush hour and summer heat. But experts tell us that the stranger was probably acting primarily out of a programmed sense of obligation that had little to do with being a good samaritan. Yet our friends believe this person willingly took an hour out of his day just to help two strangers. Similarly, evaluating behavior against the framework of your own orientation, rather than that of the actual performer, leads you to miss the real meaning and intent of what you observed.

Unlike the above, most people do not give the "beneficial" interpretation when viewing someone else's behavior against the backdrop of their commitments. Usually we give others the "half-empty" treatment rather than the "half-full" one. That is, in the proverbial bucket of life's performances, we critique others from the perspective of what they are lacking, not what they are contributing, and fail to give them the benefit of the doubt. In doing this we, in effect, hold them accountable on criteria they never had in mind to accomplish. For instance, not so long ago one of our university colleagues published a well-received book which we found very readable. In the preface, he carefully stated that his book was intended to be a practical guide for managers and professionals. Yet in reviewing it for an *academic* journal, another colleague criticized the book on grounds that it lacked scholarly citations. While this had nothing to do with the author's intent, it had everything to do with the commitments of the colleague critic who wrote exclusively for a scholarly audience and prided himself on always being "objective." It's exactly this type of situation that impedes objective evaluation on a daily basis.

People critique behavior against their own commitments, not against those of the people they are evaluating. Against the wrong frame of reference one's best accomplishments can look meager.

Thus you can see that any objective attempt to hold someone accountable must take cognizance of the self-interests involved. It must acknowledge the self-beneficial orientation of the evaluator as well as the performer. In short, it must take explicit account of alignments. Only after both alignments are understood and explicit does it become possible to grade progress objectively and measure fit. *Fit*, then, gets defined as the degree of overlap between the performer's orientation and the perspective being used to measure his or her progress. This contrasts with *adequacy* evaluations which measure the overlap between what the individual does and someone's "absolute" notion of what's needed for the organization to proceed and prosper.

---

Now don't go off thinking that we're advocating that you stand for each person doing his own thing, thereby promoting chaos. We're not. We're merely instructing you to sort out the issues of commitment from those of competence and accomplishment and to conduct constructive discussions of each. Our point is simple. There is no way of objectively holding someone accountable until the unique commitments around which that individual orients his or her work-life are understood. Evaluating someone without understanding his or her alignment produces the type of fragmentation that fuels the invisible war. Only after an individual's commitments are understood can you have real accountability, possibly in a fair way. Whether or not it is fair depends upon whether you, the evaluator, are sufficiently conscious of the personal component in your own commitments to face the possibility that there may be other equally satisfactory ways to accomplish the organization's objectives. Then the critical discussions can take place. And they probably should proceed in something like the following order.

FIRST — *Inquire into the career objectives of the person whose accountability you would like to insure.*

This is about the best way we've found for getting a slant on people's alignments and seeing the real way they orient to experience and interpret organization events. Ask for the five-year plan and then the two-year one. Find out what role their current job plays in that plan, what optimally the next step would be, whether they expect the organization to present them with that opportunity, and whatever else you need to hear in getting a fix on the unique lens that person uses in viewing daily organization life. Press people to be specific about their uniqueness. Let them know that you recognize that the same job given to ten different people is going to result in ten different jobs, each one determined by what each individual is striving to achieve.

This approach contrasts with currently used accountability techniques such as MBO (management-by-objectives) and managing-by-results. In these approaches precise contracts are made about what someone is going to produce, complete with time-tables and statements about what results are desirable and how they are going to be measured. But once stated the other person then tries to bootleg in as many self-interests as he or she can get away with and the war-of-meanings starts again. There are daily conflicts over orientation and emphasis and vigorous fights over what constitutes quality and bottom-line results.

In the approach we are advocating, accountability discussions take place on the front end, and the evaluator comes to appreciate why the performer orients the way he or she does and the unique reality in which that person lives. The tenor should be that of discussing career objectives, job demands, and self and organization fit. The idea is to get on the side of the person you are attempting to hold accountable, trying to see the world in terms of what he or she is uniquely trying to achieve. Only then can inquiries into that person's daily activities be received as constructive attempts to help rather than expressions of doubt or criticism. The idea is to get your questions of accountability received as an attempt to insure that the person as well as the organization succeeds.

SECOND — *Get a precise description of the products that person is committed to producing, complete with priorities and time-table.*

The big picture is not enough; you also need to see how what that person is endeavoring to accomplish translates into concrete organizational *products.* By products we mean tangible accomplishments, ones that can be quantified, where a direct link can be made between the individual's contribution and the organization's output. For a half-back in football, this is yards gained or touchdowns scored; for a salesman, it's orders taken or new accounts opened; for a professor, it's articles published or student evaluations of teaching; and for a production manager, it's goods out the door or reductions in damaged materials.

THIRD — *Go back over the individual's declaration of products and talk "conditions."*

By *conditions* we mean contributions that cannot be easily seen or valued but which are essential to accomplishing the thankless tasks that make organizations effective. By and large these are intangible contributions, ones which cannot be quantified, where what the individual does cannot be linked directly to the organization's outputs. For a football player, it's coaching the rookie who is being groomed to take your place; for a salesman, it's spending time with customers after the sale is made, helping them use your product efficiently even though this possibly will reduce the size of your next order. For a professor, it's counseling former students after they have graduated or turning out for graduation ceremonies after you've gotten tenure and no longer feel the need to impress. And for a production manager, it's spending additional time and thought helping other departments upgrade their performance and exercising the type of tact and support that allows them to hear your comments without becoming defensive.

FOURTH — *Review the individual's declarations of products and conditions and critique them for overlap with your own alignment—that is, with the commitments and images you are trying to advance.*

As evaluator, you don't have to be quite as candid as you need your subordinate to be. But if you are, your chances for realizing a successful performance are even greater. The more precise you are, the more likely you are to discover incompatibilities before they become problems. Of course, we're not advocating that you run out and spill your guts indiscriminately. You've got to be smart about it—candor is progressive. It requires an exchange of confidences over time and sensitivity to the specific situations in which you find yourself.

Asserting your own commitments allows you to minimize several sources of inevitable conflict.

*Initially,* it makes for a clear articulation of the conflicts that are likely to arise between the self-convenient meanings others are trying to push and meanings which are personally important to you. On the other hand, taking up these discrepancies as if you were merely motivated by a desire to do the organization's will leads to game-playing. The ironies, of course, are that no one trusts an evaluator whose motivations are not apparent, and few people are actually put off when they hear a straightforward articulation of self-interests. In either instance there will be crunch points and areas where you, even as the boss, will be forced to compromise. But you are far better off going in with these areas identified up front, or labeled as irresolvables which may or may not constitute grounds for parting company.

*Next,* identifying discrepancies between your commitments and those of the person you are evaluating helps you cope with the fact that most everyone you try to hold accountable will be skilled in playing-it-both-ways. They will be skilled in sensing your commitments and portraying their own in ways which appear to overlap. But when the moment of reckoning comes and you finally see their divergence, they are likely to cry foul by claiming that you are viewing them against a frame-of-reference that unfairly puts their commitments down.

*Next,* identifying discrepancies helps you deal in advance with the conflicts which inevitably arise over what constitutes output. Without a clear understanding of your commitments, many people will receive your assignments on terms you eventually judge to be mere inputs. Inappropriately they will carry out the letter of your instructions, not the spirit, or they will make "minor" adjustments that make a major difference to you. This is what produces the secretary who says too much or too little about your whereabouts without considering who is on the line, the engineer who does not calibrate his authoritarianism when on an assignment requiring tact and diplomacy, and the supplier who argues over who was responsible for a misshipment when you've already made it clear that you intend to pay the extra costs.

*Finally,* identifying discrepancies helps with the conflicts inevitably arising between an evaluatee's belief that your judgments are self-serving and your belief that you have the right to expect the people for whom you front to reciprocate by fronting for you. That is, everyone whose work is related to yours is part of a complex network that creates and maintains images that are essential to supporting what you are about. Having your commitments known gives people who would like to support you the opportunity to do so and people who cannot, the opportunity to disassociate themselves. Of course it also gives your enemies the ammunition they need, so pick your spots carefully.

FIFTH — *Real accountability is made possible by "before-the-fact" evaluation.*

The time to evaluate is immediately after you've reached agreement about the products and conditions the person you're attempting to hold accountable has agreed to produce. You need to assess the likelihood of that person coming through which, in part, can be predicted by how you see him or her organized to deliver today. This is not the time to be taken in by ideals. This is the time to be realistic. You want to know about the activities in which he or she is actually engaged and the ones in which he or she is not. You also want to know about the character of the relationship the person you are evaluating has formed with each of the people with whom he or she works.

You'll find that the people you are attempting to hold accountable are far more open to talking about what's less than optimum before beginning a set of tasks than afterwards. Of course, from your standpoint you know that everybody is imperfect; you merely want to check their orientation and develop confidence that they're on their way to getting better and that what's off won't produce disastrous results. Moreover, explicit dialogue about what's off on the front end can set the stage for you to position yourself on the side of the individual and against the obstacles he or she anticipates as causing problems. Then your attempts to monitor and coach can be received as needed help rather than criticism.

SIXTH — *Ask people about the development program they've created for upgrading their perceptions, relationships and competencies.*

When there's something lacking, there's something to be learned. What you want to know is whether there is concrete reason for believing that it will.

As evaluator, you'll often find yourself in the position of a father with an adolescent child. You'll see most of what needs to be learned but find that you're not always the right one to teach it. Often the best you can do is support, direct the way to other resources, and answer only those questions that are directly asked of you. Your only chance of sleeping nights will come from knowing that your child or subordinate is fraternizing with the right crowd and learning from his or her experience.

SEVENTH — *Critique results using the performer's frame-of-reference as well as your own.*

Where there is a less than optimal performance, question whether it is less than optimal in terms of the performer's self-commitments as well. If the answer is "yes," then his or her performance can be judged inadequate. If it only fails to measure up against yours, it's merely a poor fit and it is time either to review commitments, ask the person to look elsewhere for affirmation, or suggest a different job. But don't let the other person put your perspective down out of hand, particularly if you feel it is at least as good as his or hers and that you were open about it from the first.

EIGHTH AND LAST — *For whatever reason some people just don't get the message and, with them, you are better off not wasting your time.*

You'll run across an occasional instance of an individual who is so anxious, defensive and/or so focused on the organizational checklist that there is no way to get through. Once you've concluded that you've got such an instance and have tested your conclusion with the reactions of two or three others, break off the relationship. And if you've roughly followed the aforementioned steps, you can break off without guilt, knowing that you've already gone the extra mile.

Overall, this before-the-fact approach to accountability forces people to operate with increasing objectivity and produces constructive results. The focus is on helping performers to maintain the connection between their commitments and their daily activities and at the same time to build institutional supports for these commitments. It aims at the early detection of performer disorientation and of commitment conflicts between evaluators and evaluatees. It endeavors to transform ego-battering discussions of competence into ego-dignifying discussions of fit and compatibility of interests. It minimizes the mindlessness and inefficiency that can take place when people claim that the actions they are proposing for self-beneficial reasons are "objectively" required to move the organization ahead. In short, it seeks to instill a greater modicum of real objectivity into discussions of organization effectiveness by explicating the personal and subjective forces at work and treating them as realistic elements which deserve factual consideration.

◆────

Now we're set to show you specifically what our concept of before-the-fact accountability can do. We've chosen to do this with an example detailing the problems associated with getting women into the management hierarchy. This is an area in which even the most enlightened managerial approaches readily break down. Our example shows the trappings of the extant system and what we think would have been possible had our accountability principles been used. This situation was encountered by Jack, the personnel manager of a very large midwestern company.

Top-management had declared that this was the time to make an all-out effort to bring women into management and to move them up the hierarchy as quickly as possible.

Jack saw two possibilities. The first was obvious: go out and hire some female MBA's. The second was more important. Locate some smart secretaries and administrative assistants who are already on the payroll and who have university degrees and provide them the training that would make them management material. The second made sense because the company had a long-standing practice of hiring from within and Jack felt he would create resentments if there wasn't some movement from within the ranks.

After numerous discussions about how to proceed, Jack had a brainstorm. He would hire a female MBA and give her the assignment of identifying and training women who were already on the payroll. Canvassing campuses coast to coast and personally interviewing over 20 of the best applicants, Jack decided on a slim, very attractive and bright 26-year-old named Stacey. He chose her for her background in organization behavior and development, her knowledge of women's issues, and her personally engaging style. He laughed to himself, "Our managers are going to fall all over one another trying to help Stacey out."

Stacey had just completed her MBA degree—this was to be her first full-time professional job. She was very excited by the challenge and viewed this job as an excellent way to wet her feet in industry. Little did she know that this first step would take her in way above the ankles.

Jack extended a good deal of latitude in letting Stacey feel her way along. He asked her to meet with key managers to find out what they required in the way of skills and perspective for elevating females to professional and managerial positions. He also asked her to become familiar with in-company training programs and to study the range of programs used throughout industry in minority and affirmative action training. Additionally, he enrolled Stacey in the seminar series given to newly recruited male managers.

After about six months of relatively permissive supervision, Jack issued his first formal request, "Within the next couple of months, I'd like you to come up with a training program that's ready to run, as well as a formula for identifying which of our female employees have the aptitude to succeed in management." Stacey moved fast and six weeks later was ready to talk. Then, before hearing her out, Jack made a second request, "I'd like to hear about your program in the context of goal setting. Ask yourself this question: A year from now when others, including me, are looking at your performance and progress, what accomplishments will you point to and how will you substantiate that they are accomplishments?"

Jack's second question was about as good as one can do in attempting to hold someone accountable given the *current* system; let's see how it worked out.

Stacey seemed equal to the challenge. In snappy, business-like fashion her response went approximately like this: "My interviews with managers have led me to see that there is, at present, the need for two distinctly different programs, the specifics of which I'll explain in a few minutes. Program A will be run once each quarter and Program B in the fall and spring. I see three separate measures for evaluating their impact: the size of the waiting list which accumulates; the reactions of managers whose staff attends as measured by follow-up questionnaires administered three months later; and reactions of my training staff which will include what might be done to upgrade a program the next time it is given." Stacey then elaborated on the specifics of the two programs.

Jack's gut read "bittersweet" although it took an extensive conversation with us for him to conceptualize his feelings. Mostly he was conscious of his delight with the organizing skills he saw Stacey demonstrating. What alarmed him was the single-mindedness of her approach. On the one hand he would be able to hold her accountable for the perceived success of a half-dozen training programs a year. And from many perspectives this was desirable since the management development section of his personnel group was frequently asked for the numbers that justified its expense, and Stacey's effort would add numbers with relatively little additional budget.

On the other hand, Jack came to see that the bulk of Stacey's energies were about to be consumed in training programs—not necessarily to getting women elevated in the management structure. He saw how his attempt to hold Stacey accountable would lead to her supporting the status quo. He envisioned an evaluation discussion a year down the line where a confrontation about the real value of her outputs would lead Stacey to assert, "I did everything I said I would; can I help it that you've got a bunch of sexist managers who run around putting up road blocks at every turn!" And Jack thought she would have a good point. He confided, "If the truth were known, there's not much more than surface support for this program. No manager in his right mind wants to be seen as the guy who scuttled women's rights. Yet I don't dare tell her for fear of dampening her enthusiasm and opening myself up to attack if the word were to get out about what I think."

Jack, then, could point to several more dilemmas facing him down the line. *First,* Stacey herself was the symbol for women's progress and he better make damn sure of the success of her efforts. *Second,* accepting her formulation risks colluding in her eventual downfall—she doesn't have a broad view; in fact, she's operating with an accountant's formulation of career development. *Third,* to not promote her after another year would mean holding her to a tougher standard of accomplishment than anyone else at that level was currently being held to, which would not only be unfair, but would open Jack to severe criticism for utilizing a tougher standard on women than men. *Finally,* Jack saw how Stacey could succeed with her training programs, build up a big following, and he could fail because higher-ups hold him responsible for actually getting women into and through the hierarchy.

Our discussion led to Jack's seeing how the very process of accountability he had set up, using his best MBO logic, was about to do him in. And he had done all the "right" things. He gave Stacey freedom and support while establishing "objective" benchmarks for evaluating her performance. But now she's programmed to emphasize product —successful programs—to the exclusion of real accomplishment, women in managerial slots, and he's not situated to hold the discussions that might reorient her. Stacey was too far along with mean-ends activities to cope with the frustrations such a conversation would produce. How can she open-mindedly participate when the punch line is to start planning again before the programs she has designed are actually run? She needs an ancillary strategy that ensures that women who receive training are seriously considered for promotion. And tipping Stacey off about how managers truly feel makes Jack vulnerable. In her frustration, Stacey might either leak his portrayal in the wrong circles or become demotivated to the point of inactivity.

Few of the aforementioned problems would have existed had there been more before-the-fact dialogue about alignments. Most of them were the result of Jack's underestimation of how much of the problem he needed to share and how explicit he needed to be about the self-beneficial aspects entailed in his commitments. Jack's credibility depends on his being seen holding the values and commitments of the dominant corporate culture, but his effectiveness depends on getting women, beginning with Stacey, into the managerial hierarchy. But he sees most of his managers as closet sexists who need to see change as orderly and under their control. It's no accident that Stacey wound up thinking in programmatic terms after interacting with them. That's their way of playing-it-both-ways. When the time comes they can put their noses to the political winds and, if they sense lack of a critical mass, claim that they are not about to trust their important projects to people who, after all, are basically secretaries with two weeks of management training.

## Reflection

Our discussions of evaluation and accountability provide an opportunity to recap the central themes of this book.

*First,* we've characterized self-interests as the primary force that determines what goes on in organizations today. In fact, we'd go so far as to contend that the organization that takes place within each individual—what we've been calling alignment—actually determines the actions the external organization takes. To this point we feel that most students of organization behavior have been misled into thinking that one can understand organizations independently of the specific situations that specific individuals find themselves facing.

*Second,* we believe that, as they function today, organizations present people with highly politicized environments where one must engage in moment-by-moment combat in order to support and protect the images and meanings that allow them to succeed and where success is a combination of producing organization product and self-meaning.

*Third,* we've used the term "survival tactics" in characterizing the behavior people engage in when coping with the hidden self-interests of others. Although we didn't label it as such, we went into detail on the topics of evaluation and accountability because that's where the omnipresence of survival tactics seems to do most harm. People suffer from battered egos and organizations suffer from lack of excellence and creativity. We had to be prescriptive on these topics because, as organizations function today, people need better ways of protecting themselves from the disorienting demands of the system and organizations need better ways of protecting themselves from exploitation by the individual.

*Fourth,* we're deeply concerned by the specific coping strategies we see people using as they struggle with the pulls between producing *products* that the organization values and producing the *conditions* that allow themselves and others in the organization to be truly effective. Briefly, we see three stylistic tendencies: the careerist, the martyr, and the "supernigger." The careerist is the person who "successfully" produces products while cheating on his or her responsibility for producing the conditions that allow others to contribute to the overall organization effort. The martyr is the person who gets so wrapped up in conditions that he or she winds up cheating on the delivery of product. "Supernigger" is a term that came out of the minority experience of the sixties. It was used to describe the kind of double-duty effort required by those who wanted to succeed in the organization's terms while establishing the conditions that allowed others to succeed as well. Unfortunately it was only the extraordinary who had the energy and talent to pull this off and they quickly tired and became old before their time.

In contrast, what we've been advocating is a new coping style, where the focus is on alignment and a beforehand examination of self and organizational needs and priorities and a system which pays off for contributions that enable others to be more effective. Such a focus requires the full participation of both the evaluator and the evaluated with a reexamination of one's overall orientation rather than a discussion of a few finite organization tasks and products.

# 14 | A NEW LOOK AT ORGANIZATIONS

To this point we've merely dealt with the war of meanings from the perspective of the individual who wants to succeed. We've offered specific strategies for protecting against vulnerability—vulnerability to the self-serving evaluations of others and vulnerability to exploitation by those we'd like to hold accountable. But these are the short-term solutions. They do little more than provide techniques for coping with those who lack an awareness of the war of meanings, an appreciation for alignments and the need to fragment.

Now we're ready to address the longer-term solution. We know what it's going to take, a critical mass of people who think differently about organizations, and we're prepared to describe the type of educational process needed to produce them.

---

To date, most people have been trained to see organizations as external entities, separate from the minds that view them. They have been taught to present problems, facts, and frameworks in authoritative, "objective," and impersonal ways all aimed at giving the impression of rationality and objective decision making and at hiding the complex personal agenda on which these problems, facts and frameworks are based. And they've been taught to seek the same from others, even though this entails everyone working overtime to fill in the self-interests which have yet to be made apparent. The result is a population of organization inhabitants who think and communicate in externals.

This is what prompts and perpetuates the war. People fight over the meanings of external events without realizing or revealing the internal orientations that actually determine how externals get viewed and valued. Thus the categories they use in comprehending organization events are inadequate if not self-sealing, and their attempts to resolve differences in interpretation lead more to compromise and accommodation than to understanding.

As much as anything it's our system of management education that's at fault. People take courses to become more competent managers, which in their minds entails acquiring the skills to manipulate externals, and that's what they get. They seek out and are exposed to a system of thinking that pushes technical competence and the fulfillment of other people's expectations at the cost of self-reflection and considering what has personal meaning. Both at the university and on the job, managers are told what is important and how things ought to be. Seldom are they asked about their internal state. No wonder organizational inhabitants are so naive about the internal orientations that determine what is objectified and called reality.

The dynamics of education that obscure the nature of one's external orientation are vividly illustrated in a conversation Jack McDonough had with a senior partner of a Big Eight accounting firm. They were sitting next to each other at a luncheon and happened to get on the topic of executive education.

The partner mentioned that he was enrolled in the University of Southern California's Executive Development Program for Accounting Partners, a program that meets one morning a week.

McDONOUGH — How's that program shaping up?

PARTNER — It's damn good, but it makes me somewhat uncomfortable. I'm a dedicated USC alumni and I like to see their programs succeed.

McDONOUGH — Are you very far along?

PARTNER — We've just had two sessions; in fact, the last one was in your area: communications.

McDONOUGH — How did that one go over?

PARTNER — Well, that's what I mean. There was just something lacking. I walked out of there feeling it had been a waste of my time.

McDONOUGH — Was the instructor on his toes?

PARTNER — Oh, don't get me wrong. The guy gave one of the most polished presentations I've ever seen. In fact, it was more like a performance. He was really organized; he had all the principles down pat. He didn't leave one question unanswered and there were many funny asides to boot. Nevertheless, I couldn't help but feel that the session lacked substance.

McDONOUGH — What kind of feedback did you give him? (In executive education, it's customary to fill out evaluation forms after each session.)

PARTNER — That was a skillful presentation. I had to give him the highest possible rating; after all, he must have spent a week getting ready for that one session.

At this point McDonough turned silent and he says he isn't sure whether the arrival of the dessert or his state of perplexity was the cause. He had come square up against the frustration any management educator who would like to teach the lessons of inner orientations faces in thinking how to get these lessons across. Such lessons rest on teaching people to ask self-questions which have no immediate answers rather than providing them accepted answers to questions others have asked. They require self-reflection and internal confrontation which does not, at first, leave managers feeling competent and personally powerful. Here was another executive trained to admire "competence," who could not make the connection between his admiration of a smooth packaging job and what in the "educational" process bothered him. He, like the rest of us, has been taught to formulate his best questions involving personal meaning in a form that someone else can answer and then finds himself in the ridiculous position of wondering how substance, uniqueness of application, and complexity got left out.

———◆———

*What does it take to educate people about the self-interest side of their participation in organizations and, in particular, their role in creating the external organization?*

*What kind of experience will make people respectful of the personalized constructions others come up with in an attempt to make their organizational existences meaningful?*

*How can we educate large numbers of people in an appreciation for the fundamental and underlying dynamics of the organization process so that they can accept the essentials of individual alignments and act respectfully toward one another?*

Each of these questions strikes at what we believe to be the heart of the matter—conventional education lets people down. Are there alternatives? No doubt there are many and we've got one. By no means do we have ours down pat, but it seems to pick up where traditional education leaves off by teaching students how internal orientations create external organizational realities. Incidentally, we think that most of the lessons we teach are present in everyday organizational experiences and that what people really need are the skills for raising the type of self-questions that allow these lessons to be brought home to them. Consider with us how these lessons are encountered in a very challenging course we've developed for entering students in UCLA's Master's of Business Administration (MBA) program. By and large these are students with some business experience, their ages range from 22 to 50 with a median age of 27.

---

## Our Course on Internal Orientations

The lessons we have to teach are best learned through experience. So we teach this class in an off-beat manner, reasoning that the usual teacher–student model projects an order that makes certain lessons imperceivable. Our classes are small, 25 to 30 students. Rather than utilize formal assignments and lectures, we present students with a structure that violates their expectations and encourages them to reflect on how this affects them. Incidentally, our course is titled "Individual Decision Making and Complex Systems," which is sufficiently broad for us to justify almost anything, including the lessons we want to teach.

*We begin the course* with introductions and a discussion of what is involved. We tell students this is to be a "function-oriented" course with classroom topics flowing naturally from what students need to do to accomplish course assignments. Thus, we explain, nothing much is on the schedule. The course syllabus tells students that their main objective is to make this course *personally meaningful.* To this end weekly papers are assigned, in the form of personal journals, in which students are to select a particular classroom event or learning that holds significance for them and to explain why it is significant. In order to release students from the possibility of contaminating their definitions of significance and their spontaneous participation with what they think must be done to earn a good grade, we tell them that their grades will not be affected by what they write in their journals nor by what they say in class.

Students are also instructed to join with classmates of their own choosing in forming support groups in which members have the task of helping one another monitor opportunities for personal learning. As an incentive they are advised that the first one-third of their course grade will come from the average of the grades earned by the other members of their support group on a final paper discussing the meaning their journal entries hold for them. We tell them that the other two-thirds of their grade will be based on criteria which we will work out with them during class.

Directions we see as function-oriented and providing freedom are initially experienced as vague, disorienting, and lacking structure. In students' minds they have a job to do:

learn something "objective." And in past classes "objective" usually meant being able to answer on the last day of class questions they could not answer on the first, probably in the form of an exam, which provided tangible evidence that learning had been accomplished. Whether or not what they learned had personal meaning was another question. Our class addressed this "other" question.

*At the second session* we show a film and assign Culbert's book, *The Organization Trap.** The movie is a documentary depicting the dullest, most insipid aspects of organization life, with special emphasis on grovelling, political maneuvering, and impotence. Watching it provides a sharp contrast to the romanticized notions of power and autonomy which lead students to pursue the MBA degree. The book also provides a contrast. It describes how managers from top to bottom find themselves out of control precisely because they think they are in control. It contains over a hundred illustrations which students find useful in orienting themselves to the self-defeating assumptions which become the traps of organization life.

*By the end of the second week,* students find "nothing much" happening in class. The professor isn't leading, there hasn't been a discussion of the film or the book, support groups have been formed but they meet outside of class, and worst of all, the journals have been returned ungraded, leaving them with no idea of how a major part of their performance is going to be evaluated.

The students are not without the means of recourse and they retaliate. The journals become vindictive. By the third entry they've got us on the run, but their arguments entail blatant fragmentation. Rather than facing up to the inter-

* *The Organization Trap* by Samuel A. Culbert, Basic Books: New York, 1974.

nal forces involved in making this course a *personally mean-ingful experience*, they blame us for not providing the tangible external structure they expect. Bracing ourselves, we say something like, "I've read enough; I believe that most of *you* think the class is screwed, the instructor is screwed, and that you're fed up with the inference that you are in an organization trap. You've all but made a believer out of me, but I want to know one more thing. How do you reconcile your belief that you're not in an organization trap with your conclusion that all you've got to look forward to in here is thirty-two more hours of boredom when the topic is personal meaning?!"

Most students get it in class—some need a session with their support group, but eventually everybody catches on. Students realize how their belief in the external organization and their skill in the fragmentation required to perpetuate that belief has them attacking the professor rather than facing up to how out of control and helpless they feel when they can't blame externals for their disorientation. They had read about self-defeating assumptions; now they are experiencing them and, at least temporarily, realizing that it just doesn't happen to the other guy. They learn that the single most important obstacle to learning from experience is the belief that order is dictated by externals.

This experience produces new acceptance for our deviating from the conventional classroom structure, and students assume responsibility for getting sessions back on track. Speaking either as individuals or support group representatives, they begin proposing and debating procedures for having their performance evaluated. At this point we again find ourselves on the defensive, rigidly resisting attempts to have journals and classroom participation graded. We argue "functionality," stating that we don't want what we see as opportunities to learn (our organization's mission) compromised by the threat of evaluation. The debate goes on and eventually we confess that, in the service of promoting learning, we have passively sat by watching students buckle in the face of the oldest trap in the organization book. Involved is a lesson everyone knows in principle but not in practice. They've been seeking form before function, in this case, a format for deciding grades before they had determined what constituted personal meaning. We point out that whenever individuals see the organization as primarily external to them, form subverts function because the personal components of function are missing.

*It is well into the term* before students directly tackle the course objective: how to make their experiences "personally meaningful." Their first impulse is to come up with a single project that holds the same meaning for everyone. This is despite the fact that they already possess concrete evidence, in the form of journal entries describing personally meaningful classroom experiences, that each student relates differently to the same classroom events. Eventually they accept that different personal agendas for the same event are not only possible, but what inevitably takes place. Students then turn their attention to what is involved in raising the types of personal questions that can produce meaningful self-learning, questions which contrast with the circular and self-sealing logics which previously monopolized classroom conversations.

At this point, we really extend ourselves in helping students formulate what we call "open-ended" questions. These are self-searching questions which one can bring to almost any situation requiring a good deal of reflection and research and which generate learning precisely because they can't be answered quickly. For example, a student who was very active in trying to structure early class sessions, who could not sit for more than 30 seconds without saying something just to fill the vacuum created by a silent classroom, eventually asked, "Why do I need more structure?" We liked her question, but feared that it might lead to a narrow search, so we asked the class to interact with it. With some discussion, the student realized that it wasn't *any* structure she was after but *her* structure, one that was familiar enough to make her feel comfortable. On her own, she realized that it is people who bring meaning to situations and events and that this meaning is structure. She then realized that opportunities for self-learning could be found in all situations which similarly make her feel uncomfortable, where she could open-endedly question others on their relative comfort and contrast their reactions with her own. We then capitalized on her experience to underscore how understanding one's need for internal structure gives an individual greater control over the alignments he or she forms.

For another student the basis of an open-ended question spun out spontaneously during an excited classroom exchange. Again, the topic was classroom structure with discussants noting that it was not a structureless scene they were dealing with but a different, perhaps less structured, situation than they were accustomed to. At this point an intellectually oriented student who, as the son of American expatriates, had spent a great deal of time adjusting to foreign cultures, blurted out that he was so busy adjusting to the change in structure that he didn't have time to see the personal mechanisms he was using to make his adjustment. At that moment he, and the rest of the class, realized how vulnerable he was to externally imposed notions of organization and his open-ended inquiry focused on discovering the adjustment mechanisms which, in the positive sense, allow him to adapt but, because they work so fluidly, make him highly susceptible to external shaping.

Although not monitored by us, the support groups come to play an essential role in helping students learn lessons that are obscured when one thinks that organizations are

entities external to the people who view them. When someone hits a roadblock in class, behind-the-scenes coaching by
support group classmates often enables that person to see
things in another light. The support group's role in supporting in-class experimentation and personal openness
serves to document a fallacy of the external organization:
that independence and self-sufficiency are signs of personal
strength. Students find themselves needing support group
challenge and counsel in order to function open-mindedly.
Without such support, self-sealing logics take over. For example, early in the search for open-ended questions a student who had been a highly energetic classroom participant
challenged himself with what seemed to be a very appropriate self-question. He said, "I'm out to discover how to
say what's on my mind and exert the leadership I'm capable
of without pissing off people the way I've been doing here—
and elsewhere, for that matter." This seemed like a marvelous question, except his way of answering it resulted in his
keeping a low profile for the next six weeks. He "solved" his
problem by shutting up—that was self-sealing logic in action. His support group had let him down. There was just
no way for him to learn what he wanted to learn without
engaging in the conversations which used to irritate others.
Once the class caught on, he was told, "For Christ's sake,
go ahead and say something—piss us off if you have to!" He
did both. His group lent support. And he learned.

*As the term progresses*, classroom conversation develops
a graceful flow in which personal agendas intermingle with
such organization tasks as deciding the criteria for classroom achievement and how that achievement should be
measured. What is individually learned is not predictable.
That something will be learned is predictable because by
deviating from the conventional educational format, the
class allows students to perceive structural lessons that usually are too familiar to be discerned.

Inevitably there are instances of students raising what for them are important self-questions with others giving hollow responses which, in the conventional classroom, can even seem appropriate. For example, toward the end of the term a student remarked, "I've really been impressed with the close relationships I've seen formed around me and I'm wondering what I need to do to get more personally involved with others." In response, he was treated to a barrage of prescriptions. One student said, "You're too well-mannered." Another, "You need to express more confusion and uncertainty." Another, "I'd like to see you more playful." Another, "Take more risks." Another, "You've got to be less afraid of your anger." Another, "It's your attitude towards authority figures." Another, "You need to be more spontaneous." We countered, "How come everyone seems to have a solution to Bruce's problem—that is, except Bruce?" In the ensuing discussion the class recognized how our typical orientation clouds respect and appreciation for the other person's complexity. The kinds of responses Bruce received were all based on an overly simplified view of why he has difficulty opening himself to others. We saw how the way people usually think in organizations makes it possible to diminish others. For instance, someone pointed out that every organization had its "duds" and since this class is an organization of sorts, one of them must be a dud. The students all looked around nervously.

*By the end of the term*, with a little pressure and prodding from us, the class works out an imperfect evaluation scheme that both we and the students are willing to concede is a fair compromise between recognition of learning and protection from the system. For example, we can't afford to give all A's and we make this known. We explain that doing so would subject us to hostility from colleagues, whose students would pick on them for allowing our students a competitive advantage, and suspicion by the administration who, would you believe, are waging an active campaign against what they call "grade inflation." The ensuing discussion presents students with concrete evidence that our society's involvement in an external concept of organization limits people's ability to formulate a rating scheme that values their internal accomplishments. Certainly self-ratings are not sufficient because without observable product they are suspect. Besides, everyone seems to feel they've learned enough for an "A." Fortunately, those who wind up with less than "A" report that their own feelings of achievement are bolstered by an understanding of the arbitrary basis on which achievement has been measured. They see that the areas of their open-ended commitment just are not rewarded by *this* particular system.

---

How do we explain why students find these very basic lessons extraordinary? We all know most of them. What's new about learning that function must precede form, that self-questions bring meaning to experience, that overcoming self-sealing logic requires the active support of others, that people derive different meaning from the same situation, that evaluation designed to give everyone a fair chance does not necessarily give everyone the credit they deserve, and that self-affirmation is crucial to feelings of real accomplishment? Perhaps one of our lessons involves something new. It's the one that goes: we're most out of control when we think we're in control because we're only in control to the extent that our internal orientation allows us to think we are. But then this lesson is right there in the book students read. So what's the big deal?

The big deal comes in recognizing that we're all students when it comes to understanding how internal orientations create external realities. Intellectually, these are lessons we can all recite, but practically we have trouble putting them into action. At crucial junctures, our understanding gets split from our experience. For instance we can see fragmenting when we view the actions of others, but seldom when we view our own. We can be sensitive to the binds others create for us and not see how what we do to resolve our binds contributes to binds which cause others to grope for survival tactics as a means of saving their own organizational life. Worst of all, relating primarily to an external organization causes us to buy into absolute definitions of commitment and responsibility. We expect rational logic and objective performance even though we also know that someone's actions can never be viewed independently of their interests and their highly personal construction of reality.

## 15 | A NEW LOOK AT POWER

Most people are accustomed to defining power as the ability to direct, control, and influence others. However, given what we now know about alignments, we can see that this is a limited view. In fact, this is probably the least interesting way to think about power.

Real power has more to do with clearing space for your own interests than getting others to perform in a certain mode. It has less to do with having a position which allows you to give orders than with being able to present what is personally important in a publicly creditable way. Certainly most people can cite examples of someone who had plenty of license to boss, reward, and punish, but who lacked the ability to sense or achieve personally meaningful goals. Many in the Nixon White House clearly fell into this category. No, we've been misled into thinking that power has to do with exerting control over others. It has far more to do with exercising control over ourselves.

To be more precise, we think popular notions of power should be expanded to include *the power that results from having an effective alignment as well as the organizational images which give you the credit for using it.* Such power depends on knowing yourself well enough to stay self-oriented and on knowing how to get your contributions to the organization seen and valued. It also depends on knowing how to block others and hold them off when you sense that the interpretations they are pushing will make life more difficult for you.

Thus we believe that in today's mode of operating, real power accrues to those who are able to go out into the public arena and successfully lobby for organizational images that support what they are personally about, while remaining inwardly connected in the face of a never ending series of negotiations with those whose alignments cause them to want reality defined in competing ways. It entails surviving the war of meanings with one's sense of self-purpose intact.

The power that comes from an effective alignment emanates both from a sense of personal meaning and organizational contribution. Few people are satisfied when they find they lack either component. Organization lives lack punch when one pursues self-interests without producing payoffs for the institution, and people feel like objects when engrossed in grinding out organization product without producing much that has personal meaning. You can tell when you're without an effective alignment when you find yourself feeling dissatisfied with your job, either because you are not learning and are going too long between periods of excitement or because you find your real aptitudes and talents not utilized in the tasks required to perform your job effectively.

While an effective alignment is a necessary component of organization power, it is by no means a sufficient one. Everyone knows people who function with relatively uncompromised personal values and high responsiveness to the needs of the organization but whose talents and contributions are not adequately valued. These are people who have effective alignments but who lack power because they have been unsuccessful in erecting a set of images that allow them to pursue their alignment with credibility. Either they lack image management skills or are naive to the essential battles each person must fight. Certainly this was the problem Nancy, the education director described in Chapter 6, faced when she picked up responsibilities for the national convention. She knew she lacked the experience to do a great job, but she felt she had the talents to do a creditable one, and she saw an opportunity to fill a crucial organizational void and to learn at the same time. But Nancy neglected to erect the images necessary to get appreciation for what she was seeking to do and her contribution went unappreciated. She was merely criticized for all the tasks left undone while she was trying to perform two jobs at once.

When it comes to erecting images to support one's alignment, most people resort to what we've been calling survival tactics. Survival tactics offer a familiar and dependable way to get self-convenient definitions of mission, role and daily activities accepted by the organization. People frame, fragment, and play-it-both-ways in the service of getting others to go along with those interpretations of organizational happenings which support what they are about. To review how useful and, at the same time, how destructive survival tactics can be, we'd like to tell you about one of the most artful strategists we've observed.

Carl, a senior partner in one of Los Angeles' largest law firms, knows the tactics well and applies them skillfully. He has a sensational alignment, one that features his expertise in tax law and which portrays him as a benefactor to young lawyers on the rise. This, not so incidentally, has the effect of surrounding Carl with apprentices who are only too happy to do scuff work in exchange for the opportunity to learn from the master.

A good deal of Carl's success can be credited to an impression he fosters that an apprenticeship in his tax department not only provides tax expertise but furthers one's career in the firm. Unfortunately for young lawyers who desire partnership this isn't always true. Carl pretends to give much more support than he actually delivers. The fatherly-sponsor image he promotes comes at the expense of his proteges' autonomy and separate identity. A young lawyer must be sure to credit the master, do it his way and pay homage on a daily basis. Otherwise, Carl's behind-closed-doors support falls quite short of the face-to-face statements of fatherly concern he gives in the corridors. (And can Carl ever give the corridor performances!)

A recent example of such an inauthentic performance came just the other day when Carl met up with Mike, a young lawyer who had moved on from a period spent working with Carl to apprenticeships with partners in different specialties. At the time Mike moved on he paid Carl his tribute, but Carl understood that Mike's desire to move had as much to do with his unwillingness to defer to him as it did with his interests in other facets of law. Nonetheless, Carl wished him the best and told anyone who would listen that Mike's moving on merely bespoke of a young man's desire to have a less specialized practice. But when it came time for the firm's partners to privately debate Mike's acceptability for partnership, Carl's true feelings came out.

After a fierce fight Mike did get promoted. But the debate stretched out several weeks and in the service of keeping Mike's anxiety at a tolerable level, several partners leaked the news that Carl was representing Mike's tax work as something less than acceptable. Publicly this presented

Carl with an image problem. Should word get around that this fatherly benefactor turns on those who fail to identify with him, his organization image would be tarnished and he would lose organizational support for his alignment.

Well, you can imagine the corridor performance Carl had to give the first time he met up with Mike after the news got out that Mike had successfully scaled the wall to partnership. Carl was at his best and gave an artful demonstration of spontaneous framing, fragmenting and playing-it-both-ways. Read what was transacted and see if you don't agree.

CARL — You seem very happy, I'm delighted about that. Let's be sure to get together soon to talk about your future. You know I just sat in those meetings stunned, puzzled by all the lousy things they were saying about you.

MIKE — I got the story a little differently, I'm surprised to hear you say you're delighted.

CARL — I was stunned. With all that criticism, I just couldn't help but think that you'd be better off someplace else. In fact, I figure now's a good time for you to leave. You can use your partnership with our firm to get a first-rate position wherever you like.

MIKE — Come on Carl, lots of the partners had a tough time getting through, and they're all right today.

CARL — Oh, you're missing my point. I'm not concerned about future opportunities; I'm concerned that your feelings about the struggle will block your creativity and expression today. Those other guys didn't have any creativity to be blocked. You have enormous potential and I'd like to see you working where your talents can be better appreciated and nurtured. Let's have a long talk soon.

Of course, there never was a long talk—the images were in place. But there were many replays of these corridor words as Carl spread the story that his unwillingness to give strong support to Mike's case was based on his fear that the ability to maintain a constructive approach of someone as sensitive as Mike would be eroded after such an emotionally trying promotion. In fact, Carl let it be known that it was because he cared so much that he couldn't come out and support Mike. His critical comments behind closed doors? Oh, he wasn't trying to knock Mike off, he was merely trying to get other critics out in the open so that the specifics of their criticisms could be invalidated before the vote. To this day Carl contends he had no concern about Mike's ability, just about whether there's adequate appreciation in the firm for such a "generalist."

———————◆———————

Do you like it? Did you like what took place when someone artful in deploying survival skills goes about creating the images that support his alignment and displaying personal power? Well we don't like it either. But frankly, we feel humble in the face of the practicality of using such an approach. In today's organizational world survival tactics are the sure-fire way to clear space for an alignment. Those who use them, like Carl, succeed and prosper; those who don't—fail, even if they have worthy purposes and organizationally functional self-interests. In most of today's organizational world, the pursuit of personal power is synonymous with the reality controlling tactics of framing, fragmenting, and playing-it-both-ways.

### Our Alternative

Now we must declare ourselves. This book was not written to present an imperative for survival tactics and to provide a primer aimed at helping our readers to out-frame, out-fragment, and out-fox those who have yet to catch on to what is taking place beneath words of professed objectivity. We recognize how essential image management is, and we seek an alternative to self-expression tactics which come at another's expense. We seek an alternative to the war of meanings—to people having to shade reality while contending that what they advocate is chosen primarily on grounds of what is objectively required to move the organization ahead.

*In our view, what people advocate is constrained by, not chosen for, its ability to move the organization ahead, and the extreme costs associated with the war of meanings should include self-deception and self-disorientation right along with one's deception of others.*

We have identified an alternative to today's use of survival tactics in clearing space for alignments—an alternative that reaps considerable power for those who become skilled in using it. Like the other proposals we've offered, this alternative relies on conscious recognition of the fact that personal alignments direct people's activities and interpretations of organizational happenings. It's an alternative that is being used by a handful of organization players and perhaps when we describe it you'll associate it with someone you know. Among the people we know who use it, Colin is our favorite.

Colin's power comes from three sources:

1. An effective alignment.
2. An ingrained respect for others and their right to be personally expressive.
3. A deep-seated belief that each person lives a unique reality, what we've been contending in our use of the term *alignment.*

In other words when there is a clash or an organizational disappointment, Colin is the cool head who comes in to figure out why the clash or inept performance took place.

In fact, that's his job now. He's the top-level trouble-shooter for a conglomerate that owns over thirty smaller companies.

Now Colin is human too. Like the rest of us, his first impulse in hearing of an action that gets in the way of a course he is pursuing is to run down there and straighten the son-of-a-bitch out. But unlike most of us, he quickly moves on to a more sober place. Almost always he frames his concerns in a form that essentially inquires: "What could lead a well-intentioned, bright, highly motivated person like this to operate in the dysfunctional way I've just observed?" Given Colin's minority experience as a child, this is a genuinely held question, not a technique. What a difference it makes when someone comes in obviously unhappy with the action you've taken but clearly communicating that he's not about to propose something else until he understands how your course of action or proposed perspective lines up with the inner framework that led to its pursuit. What's more, Colin's approach is terribly effective in getting the other person to sit still for a comparable perspective on Colin. That is, Colin gets others to listen to his interests, which he communicates in a no-nonsense manner, and then earnestly inquires how a better matchup could be created.

Colin seldom states his interests in anything that could be considered unusually selfish, which is a real plus in his approach. His brilliance lies in the intuitive way he communicates just enough background to give the person with whom he's negotiating a feel for what he has personally at stake. He seldom reveals specifics that could get him labeled as anything but a fairminded statesman, which, incidentally, we see not only as a politically important restraint but as a blind spot of Colin's. Our discussions with him leave us feeling that Colin's awareness of other people's self-interests, and their right to pursue them, does not extend to himself. He endeavors to live an exemplary life which sometimes causes his associates guilt as they realize they are nowhere near as selfless as Colin appears to be.

No, Colin is not always successful in establishing compatible interests and his willingness to see a situation through his adversaries' eyes sometimes gets interpreted as his being played for the fool. But when you stop and reflect, it's not hard to understand why Colin's approach is, by and large, so effective. Not only does he seem to succeed in finding common ground on about three out of five occasions where sharp differences exist, but in a high proportion of the remaining instances individuals gain respect both for his perspective and the approach he uses. As a result, they are willing to check out future actions with him before committing publicly to a competing course of action.

What about the residual group of compulsive power seekers who are so firmly entrenched that they cannot or will not negotiate reality and insist that every issue be debated on the battlefield of meanings? How does Colin deal with this set of individuals? Again, Colin is the statesman. He is not prideful about the number of times he must give the other guy the benefit of the doubt in working toward an appreciation of each other's interests. While it is possible to reach common agreement with some individuals in one sitting, Colin recognizes that it may take six months to a year with others. He wants to be very sure that there is no room for negotiation before he drops adversaries into the "incorrigible" category where he no longer extends the courtesy of a "friendly" reading of their actions. And when he takes aim at someone, that person better watch out. Incorrigible power seekers find that years of seeking out others at their strongest rather than weakest points provide Colin a network of sympathizers who see his tactics as constructive to the wider interests of the corporation and who are inclined to give all the close calls to him.

Now we can list the steps we're advocating as an alternative approach to the use of survival tactics in clearing space to pursue one's alignment. We've identified eight although probably, knowing our principles, you'll think of others.

> FIRST — *Recognize, appreciate, and remain conscious of the fact that there is no way of comprehending the rationale behind someone's behavior, or "objective" presentation of the facts, until you understand the alignment that underlies that person's orientation.*

This is particularly important to remember when someone takes an action or promotes a meaning that rubs against the grain of your orientation. Resist the impulse to immediately set that person or situation straight. Instead inquire further for the perspective that makes this orientation reasonable.

> SECOND — *Knowing the other person's alignment is not sufficient, having the other person know that you know is essential.*

Only when people know that you see their actions in the context of what they are trying to achieve uniquely (their alignment), and understand some of the personal history that makes what they are pursuing personally meaningful, is there a chance that they will open themselves to what you are about and genuinely consider compromise.

> THIRD — *Provide others a personal perspective on what you are trying to accomplish and the importance it holds in terms of what matters to you (your alignment), and what your work unit is trying to accomplish (its mission), but do not fill in the obvious.*

That is, give others the specifics to develop a perspective on what has personal meaning to you and what organizational contribution you are trying to effect, but *do not* make the final connections that would allow others to specify a specific self-beneficial or self-indulgent action that you've taken. No doubt they will make such connections on their own, but don't let them come from you. Ridiculous as it sounds, today's organization mind has a limited capacity to tolerate the self-indulgent, and more progress will have to be made before you can safely remove the last vestige of false objectivity and trust people to accept your interests without moral indignation.

> FOURTH — *Do not, after revealing your alignment, grab control by immediately proposing an alternative course of action.*

Let the other person sit a while with your perspective. This will communicate a desire for moving from the marketplace of competing realities to a place where work associates search for mutually compatible solutions. Try to avoid self-righteousness. To you it may seem that what you are advocating benefits more people and affords more productivity for the organization, but also keep in mind that the reasons for your proposal are no less self-serving than the reasons behind what the other person is advocating. What's more, in organizations, debates are not decided on virtue alone, they are decided primarily on which alternative does the most for the alignments of other key players. This is not to say that you should not go all out in the expression of personal values and take a stand against actions and perspectives you find offensive. But it does mean that in instances where self-interests, and not deep personal values are involved, your first objective lies in finding a win-win solution for a conflict which was initially formulated win-lose.

> FIFTH — *Try to negotiate with the objective of adding a person to the network of people who respect you for fair-play and at some future time will be inclined to give you and your point of view the benefit of the doubt.*

Once you and the other person learn enough about one another's interests to conclude that a win-win solution is not possible, stop with all that objectivity and find out who has what to give. Someone has to miss Christmas dinner to fly to the snows of Poughkeepsie in time to make a December 26th sales meeting. At this point we recommend a secondary strategy, because there's no long-term percentage in holding out for the other person to go. It's a fact that the sacrifice is going to fall to someone and it's essential that the sacrifice be recognized and reciprocated. Once a conflict has gotten this far don't bother with all those organizational imperatives, you couldn't fool your own grandmother.

> SIXTH — *If you can't uncover a mutually compatible solution and you're going out to take a unilateral course that the people you've been negotiating with are not going to like, make sure you signal them in advance.*

If you fear their knowing will allow them to beat you to a scarce resource or tell a story that diverts people from the appeal of your proposal, then back up and tell them something more abstract about what you are going to do so that later on they do not feel betrayed believing you told them one thing and did another. The principle here is simple. Play by an ethical, nonduplicitous code long enough and most others will reciprocate, at least to the extent to which they are capable.

> SEVENTH — *Try to minimize the extent to which you take an irresolvable conflict or competing orientation personally.*

In the organizational world there are political contingencies that bear on even the closest of friends. While it is a fact that every issue personally impacts on you, try to see that in most cases what the other person is doing relates primarily to his or her alignment and would be invoked in almost any situation

in which someone like you presents him or her with a similar
dilemma.

EIGHTH — *Remember alignments are themes which are
constantly being revised as an individual experiences new
situations and learns more about the realities others live.*

Focusing on alignments, using the fact that they exist as a
starting point for appreciating the rationality behind the other
person's apparent irrationality, and hearing what the other
person has to say about you present unusually rich sources of
learning and feedback relative to upgrading the quality of
your personal goals and orientation to the organization world.

———————◆———————

Admittedly the approach we've just proposed is born out of
values, not short term pragmatics. An effective alignment and
a supporting set of organizational images are essential. That is
pragmatic. Without them one lacks a brand of power that is
so crucial that the lack of it calls into question all other brands
of power. But how one goes about creating organizationally
acceptable statements of mission, role and daily activities is a
matter of personal values. Whether you choose to accept that
people have the right to differentially relate to the task requirements of their jobs in an effort to maximize the expression of self-interests and that the overall organization effort
suffers when people covertly pursue self-interests by attempting to take control of the realities others live, or whether you
reason that you didn't invent the game, you merely came to
play it to win, is a matter of values.

Those who choose our alternative will, no doubt, find that
their effectiveness in using it depends on practice. You can't
expect to emulate Colin's style with the same degree of success
he enjoys without suffering some hard knocks at first. After all,

most of the other guys are playing by a different set of rules. They are clearing space using survival tactics which have stood them well over the years. Otherwise they would not have gotten so far. Nonetheless, our research and personal experience have produced ample evidence that explicit acknowledgement and appreciation for other people's alignments by even a handful of people in the same organization begins to shift that institution's culture. However, producing that handful, a critical mass of people whose daily practice begins to turn their organization around, requires more than people with skills, it requires a new type of leadership. It requires leaders who accept the inevitability of self-interests and who, however instinctively, understand enough about alignments to help their subordinates modify their relationships to the system, to others in their work group, and to other organizational units.

# 16 | A NEW LOOK AT LEADERSHIP

"My boss, Chuck, is my biggest help and at the same time my biggest hindrance. His impatience and brilliance are always in my way. He calls instant meetings that break my daily flow and there's no telling when he's about to steal my biggest problem. All my people from lathe operators to shift foremen run to his office at their slightest whim. He's better informed about my operation than me; that is, about what's going wrong! I told my guys not to talk with him but he got wind of it and chewed my ass. He says I ought to know what's going on at all times and that it's my fault when I don't.

"Then we have these team meetings. I almost started to

count on them until he began to cancel them whenever he failed to see something on the agenda that interested him. When am I going to initiate? Certainly it's not when Chuck is on the loose.

"Now he is right a great percentage of the time, oftentimes fair, and very generous with the bucks. On the other hand, he has no reluctance to read a manager out in public, anywhere in front of his people, even in the washroom. Then it's a one-way pronouncement, not a two-way exchange.

"The end result is that I spend a good portion of my day thinking 'what would Chuck do,' even before I think about what needs to be done. He's usually right, so I've got that going for me. What's more, that way I stay out of trouble."

———————◆———————

We know Chuck; and this statement, made by his manufacturing manager, bears out our experience. Chuck exemplifies the pseudo-style of *charismatic* leadership that most managers try to achieve. But only the very smart one can pull it off because its success rests on always being right and on overpowering impossible situations. Once in a rare while someone like Gandhi walks through who exudes real charisma. Most people fall somewhat short of Gandhi, but they are revered nevertheless for their effectiveness in getting jobs done, running organizations, and "leading" people. In the conventional sense Chuck is a true leader; there's no question about that. He's the guy who got the cameo treatment in his company's annual report for single-handedly turning a faltering company around. Of course, the Chuck statements included in the report attributed it all to a "team-effort," No, in our estimation it was single-handed. Chuck ordered and shoved, cut and screamed, and brought in the type of wisdom and discipline that produced an efficient operation with profits to spare. However, as you can see from the introductory soliloquy, his mode of leadership also produced the kinds of dilemmas which cause people to frame, fragment, and play-it-both-ways.

Of course people use survival tactics when dealing with the Chucks, Kissingers, Gineens, and Paleys of the world. Such leaders appear to have little tolerance for a subordinate who expresses an inner logic that doesn't parallel their own. What's more, they seem to operate in a way that's guaranteed to weaken the effectiveness of anyone who insists on pursuing an alternative orientation. Invoking schisms is the only way competent underlings can hold out for what's personally meaningful while delivering what these leaders believe to be organizationally effective. All orientations must be camouflaged to match the ones of the leader. Hence the illusion of charisma. And because these leaders are so effective they attract a large following. People are enticed by a beguiling fantasy. They fantasize having sufficient control of how situations and problems are defined that their approach will always be effective. What's more, such power promises to make one invulnerable to the daily war of meanings. When there's a conflict the other guy will be wrong—by definition.

Nevertheless, there is good news on the horizon. Increasing numbers of us are groping for an alternative. Our instincts and intuition carry us toward an orientation that contrasts sharply with Chuck's. We sense the arbitrary and self-beneficial aspects of our own participation and look for ways to respect these components in the actions of others—without compromising our own organization effectiveness in the process. But because what we do deviates from what people expect, we never seem to stimulate more than an ambivalent reception. For instance, consider the following statement made about a senior level manager whose leadership style is quite different from Chuck's.

"If Fred were six foot six and weighed 250 pounds his style would be fabulous. But he's a shrimp and doesn't give us enough of what we're looking for. Our managers constantly criticize him for not making decisions. Asking him for the bottom line becomes a test of patience. He likes to analyze and ask questions which put you off balance. But for some reason, hidden to me, people come out of his office knowing exactly what to do and without being told.

"He says his job is to do whatever it takes to keep the ship moving in a satisfactory direction. But just once I'd like to hear him tell us where the ship is going. I've told him as much and he says *we* know damn well where we're going and that frequently our idea is better than his. And he can cite examples.

"To his credit he meets regularly with each of us who are his subordinates and he really puts in the hours. However, much of his time is spent on external relations. He's always talking with higher-ups and is willing to sit down with just about anyone with whom our division interacts. I've never heard him raise his voice with one exception, and then it was with the fiercest of our senior directors. It was a meeting of our entire executive committee and this director was really coming off the wall. Finally Fred banged his fist on the table, just like in the movies, and said, 'For the last hour we've told you in fifty different ways that we're doing the best we can given what we face, and you keep going as if you haven't heard our facts. In case you haven't gotten the point, let me say it again: your idea of perfection pays no attention to what we're up against.' That guy stopped dead in his tracks and apologized. The word got around, and for the next week people treated Fred as if he were six foot fourteen, even though he hadn't grown an inch."

At best it's an uphill battle for those leaders who have Fred's instincts and want to survive. First, these leaders' instincts lead them to a style that goes against what others expect. Second, others lack the categories for recording the special things these leaders attempt to do. If the so-called "charismatic" leader causes problems because he or she declares what is "reality" and forces people to fragment, then Fred's style causes problems because people are accustomed to using survival tactics which, unless someone asserts what reality is, leaves them feeling unsure of what direction they are taking.

Most of us have been socialized to desire a leader who asserts a structure and makes endlessly wise decisions. What we don't accept is that few leaders are actually that wise. Their apparent wisdom is the result of operating within a structure that is rooted in their own alignment. Few of us know how to respond to a leader whose core concern lies in clearing space for us to assert a direction that best taps our competencies and who values how we want to contribute to the organizational effort. We are far more accustomed to having the structure laid out for us and to bootlegging self-interests in on the side.

Now the scene is set for us to be precise in describing the kind of leadership we advocate. It's a style of leadership that seeks to direct and manage the self-beneficial interests which underlie people's participation at work. It's a style that recognizes the uniqueness of each individual's alignment and the inner organizations which different alignments produce. As we said before, it's a style of leadership that some people perform intuitively but, because the categories for appreciating its outputs don't exist, its value to the organizational effort goes unnoticed. But how could these categories exist? People barely recognize the war of meanings or the participation style that they use in surviving it.

Our idea of effective leadership emphasizes three activities: counseling, team-building, and brokering. Each is aimed at helping others to be powerful—helping others to clear the space they need to assert themselves in directions which maximize personal, career, and organizational accomplishment and which lessen the need for schisms. Each is a condition-setting function that allows people to deliver in areas of greatest excellence while holding them accountable for quality and accomplishment. Unfortunately, within today's scheme of things, counseling, team-building and brokering are activities best noticed when missing and seldom prized when present. Bosses who perform them are missed far more when they are gone than they are valued when they are around.

---

### Counseling

In industry the word "counseling" is often interpreted as a handholding activity in which leaders converse sympathetically with subordinates and make fun of them later on. This is not the kind of counseling we have in mind. Ours is an explicit discussion of alignments and careers in an effort to understand the unique definitions of commitment and responsibility that orient an individual. The counseling is aimed at establishing whether a fit can exist between what the individual finds personally meaningful and what the organization needs from that individual. Thus it also includes familiarizing the individual with the expectations of others in the organization and the other self-beneficial interests involved.

Often an individual will encounter problems in getting his or her work valued by the organization. Then the counseling involves diagnosing and analyzing the problem of having it valued, and conceptualizing the mismatch between what the individual seeks self-beneficially and what the organization needs to have done. In our terms it's an alignment that isn't working, and the leader has the job of exploring alternatives that might produce a better fit. When none is available it's up to the leader to portray it as a poor fit, not an inadequate performance.

We've already said a good deal about the specifics of evaluation and accountability and much of it is relevant here. We said it makes no sense to talk task, product, and conditions, until you first understand the unique angle of personal meaning and career success that characterizes what someone is trying to achieve. Leaders such as Chuck ignore this step and try to seize each intimate encounter with a subordinate as a chance to slip in a set of images aimed at benefiting themselves, often at the subordinate's expense. If you are tempted to do this recall the preceding sections of this book in which we presented a number of vignettes to illustrate the infinite resourcefulness of the people you seek to control. And there's much more to fragmentation than we've covered in our discussion.

All of this advice, however, is subject to a basic contingency. In fact, you can scrap everything we've just said when counseling a person who is programmed to compromise his or her own definition of success when facing a discrepancy between what the organization seems to value and what he or she has produced. This is the person who reasons that since what they really want most is success in the organization, then no compromise is really a compromise. This is a self-deceiving mentality that's already been covered in a previous volume, *The Organization Trap*, and we refer readers who want to learn more about self-defeating behavior in organizations to that book. Back to the point of this discussion, the leader's role includes encouraging people to hold the searching self-dialogues that precede their self-portrayals to others.

---

### Team-Building

Most leaders who engage in team-building do so out of a recognition that improved rapport and communications among those reporting to them will result in higher quality decisions and enhanced integration of the total work effort. They understand that division of labor and diverse expertise requires open communications and teamwork. What few realize is that you can have open communications and not be talking about the right things. If anything, this book should have convinced you that people just are not talking about the issues that most determine their participation and their view of what is taking place. Roy thought A and said Y, Cantrell thought B and said Z, and then the two of them argued over which was superior, Y or Z. That's why the three-minute decision required a number of two-hour meetings. The goal of real team-building is to reduce the debate to a single 45-minute one.

Current notions of team-building need to be expanded to include an appreciation of what peers, bosses, and subordinates are trying to accomplish personally and professionally and to legitimatize their right to look for ways of accomplishing this while taking care of organizational responsibilities. The leader's job is to get subordinates to relate to one another based on a recognition that each person holds self-beneficial interests which create a particular orientation to their job.

As we mentioned in Chapter 5, we've done some experimenting in which we ask a boss and his or her subordinates to informally state for one another the personal, professional and career goals they would like to achieve within the next five years. To date the results have been highly gratifying.

*First*, getting a glimpse of the internal orientation that the other person uses allows people to work more efficiently with one another. Each individual gets a better sense of how to approach others in order to get a credible hearing.

*Second*, knowledge of the other person's alignment allows people to effectively cue one another when they sense that the other person is lost in the moment and not operating in a way that serves either their cause or the organization's.

*Third*, knowing that the other person has an understanding

of your motivations leads to less deception and fewer false assertions of objectivity.

*Fourth*, knowing the ingredients of someone else's alignment seems to generate support for that person's projects and respect for that persons pursuing meaning in a way that's consistent with his or her self-assessment and ego ideal. This reduces the war of meanings and attenuates the loneliness endemic to organization life.

*Fifth*, and best of all, knowing something as intimate as the particulars of another person's alignment seems to convey a sense of obligation whereby peers actively attempt to create the conditions that support the other person's raising of the open-ended questions necessary for upgrading his or her internal orientation.

---

## Brokering

Most leaders already spend a fair amount of time brokering their organization's interests in the marketplace of competing images. Externally they are their organization's link to the next level of institutional integration, and internally they are the reconnaissance unit charged with bringing in the perspectives that keep their organization viable. But given how things operate today, this role involves a great deal of fragmentation.

Leaders who understand that people's reactions to the external organization depend on what people have personally at stake and who appreciate the essentiality of unique alignments will perform the brokering role with much less duplicity. On the external side, they will be far more concerned with creating the images that allow their group to be valued and appreciated where they are uniquely strong, than they will be in portraying their organization's product as scoring on dimensions a particular critic values. On the internal side, they will be far better focused on questioning their group

members about how their individual contributions relate to
group-level commitments than they will be in critiquing individual product against an abstract and overly idealized notion of perfection. Their score-keeping standard will emphasize "degree of fit," not "degree of adequacy." Their first
score-keeping question will be about orientation; their second
will be about accomplishment in the orientation that has just
been discussed; their third will be about how what has been
produced matches with the external expectation; and their
fourth will be about the measures necessary for narrowing the
gap between what external groups desire and what seems internally correct.

Thus we envision a brokering role in which leaders take an
active hand in candidly educating external audiences about
the unique capabilities and products their organizations can
deliver. First and foremost, the leader needs to discuss mission; then the unique slant that distinctively identifies the
roles his or her organization can ably play in the pursuit of
this mission; and finally the scope of activities that, in his or
her mind, constitute the operation of this role and mission.
The latter is most important because, by definition, external
constituencies hold different alignments and will always require a roadmap to appreciate contributions coming from
orientations that are different from their own.

Internally we envision a brokering role in which leaders encourage group members to discuss team mix—who blocks for
whom, what personal needs must be deferred in favor of someone else's, and how the organization can be more responsive
to messages received from external groups.

To date we've done only a moderate amount of experimenting with our formulation of brokering, but our results give us
reason for high optimism. By and large we find that external
critics respond well to straightforward statements of organization competence and are very willing to constructively discuss the tradeoffs involved in alternate orientations. By telling

a story which candidly describes team capabilities, but does not reveal what the external audience is prepared to judge as the inadequacies of individuals, we've seen work-group leaders succeed in getting other departments to buy a set of commitments and expectations of output on the front-end that closely parallel what his or her group is uniquely equipped to deliver. We have not yet gotten very far in testing this approach with constituencies external to one's own organization or in the public sector where a more entrenched adversary relationship is involved. For instance, in our vignette about mental health in California, we wonder about the type of candid approach a Los Angeles County mental health director could use in pursuing a budget increase that would prove persuasive to the governor during an election year.

---

## CONCLUSION

It's appropriate that we've saved our favorite story for the end. It's a story about a manager who embodies the best of both the subjective and the rational approaches to leadership and for us is a symbol that it can be done. This manager is able to go toe to toe with hard-boiled characters like Charlie and at the same time remain sensitive to the contributions made by leaders like Fred. He's a manager who searches for ways of relating to the uniqueness of those reporting to him while he shuns calling "objective" that which he sees as arbitrary and a matter of personal convenience.

The manager we have in mind demonstrated the effectiveness of much that we are advocating in three distinct settings: industry, education, and public service. First, he fought his way through the highly competitive world of consumer products where he became Chairman of the Board of one of the nation's largest and most successful conglomerates. Next, in the educational field, he became the dean of a large and prestigious professional school, instituting changes that brought national recognition to that institution. And most recently he was the President's choice to head a world-renowed agency and this appointment brought instant acclamation from the Senate Hearings Committee. All this took place before his forty-seventh birthday!

In our view the key to this manager's success lies in his ability to see the connection between personal effectiveness and organizational efficiency. To him, these are highly related issues. He believes that organizations exist to serve people, not the other way around, and he constantly searches to understand what people are trying to achieve in the way of personal meaning and career success. Nevertheless, his style is one which frequently gets misinterpreted as soft and permissive leadership and does not produce an easy route to universal love and appreciation. His understanding of personal projects allows him to penetrate many of the facades people construct, and this makes him the target of behind-the-scenes ambivalence and face-to-face suspicion. Let's examine his impact more closely.

In the first place, he resists spending the bulk of his energies responding to problems defined by others as "crises." This orientation allows him to take tough stands with respect to the succession of "crises" any top administrator faces, and which, if passed down through the organization, can make it impossible for anyone to align self-interests with the task requirements of their job in a way that's constructive for the institution. In the short run his "nonresponsiveness" makes him vulnerable to the charge that he is not on top of a situation. In the long run, however, he frees himself and the people in his organization from the oppressive burden of always responding to someone else's firedrill.

We certainly don't want to mislead you into thinking that our hero, or any other leader, could emerge from each of these settings totally unscarred. To the contrary, on his way to the board chairmanship he spent more than three years going eyeball to eyeball with a manager whose style was the antithesis of his own and whose subordinates consider him to be "the biggest prick you're ever going to find in a chief executive's office." When our leader realized that he was going to be locked in mortal combat for as long as he stayed with the conglomerate, he began to look around. That's when he got into education. Some say things got too hot for him to handle. In our minds his decision revealed that he saw more to life than surviving corporate death struggles.

It's interesting to contrast the subordinates who value his leadership style with those who don't. Those who see flexibility in the construction of their own alignments generally appreciate his style. But he causes fits among those with careerist and martyr mentalities. These people are confused by his respect for the personal side of their alignments. They mistake his sensitivity to what is personally meaningful to them as agreement with their self-beneficial formulations of what the organization needs to do. Consequently they experience small betrayals when learning of a decision he takes after surveying their perspective. What they don't understand is that our hero seriously considers competing perspectives prior to making a decision and that his integration is almost always original, with even the people who influenced him the most finding themselves unable to identify their input in what he prints out. But for those with open-ended questions, his printouts are almost always educational. By factoring out what he added, they deduce what this leader sees as the limitations in their formulations.

For almost everyone, his style is disarming. His searching respect for the subjective side of an individual's participation is responded to as a warm and irresistible invitation to tell all. This makes it quite difficult to fragment. Knowing that he knows their subjective interests causes most people to tell their whole story—either out of a fear of looking stupid or one of getting caught telling a half-truth. In subtle ways this leader conveys the message that he's not there simply to serve the self-indulgent needs of individuals but to provide another perspective on what the organization needs and to challenge people to find a more synergistic means of relating their needs to organization product. And he's been able to do this and still score on the traditional checklist.

In many ways this leader is bigger than life; certainly his accomplishments surpass what most of us are externally striving to achieve. Today's society seems to worship external success, yet each of us knows that we're up to so much more. Our hero often strikes us as a very lonely man and we can't help but think that a major part of what appears to be a self-imposed solitude derives from an understanding that, in today's world, his accomplishments are valued for reasons which bear little resemblance to what he sets out to do. But help should be on the way. We believe the evaluation categories which convey illusions of objectivity and overemphasize externals will gradually change. And as more people demonstrate an enhanced appreciation for the subjective involvements that everyone brings to organization life, this leader, together with the rest of us, will have an easier time being himself and gaining recognition for just that.

# INDEX

**223**

**About the authors...**

SAMUEL A. CULBERT is Professor of Behavioral and Organizational Science at UCLA's Graduate School of Management. He is one of a rare breed of clinical psychologists who hold full-time management professorships at major universities. Well-known for his writings on organizations and the individual's struggle for success and meaning at work (he is author of THE ORGANIZATION TRAP), Dr. Culbert is also an authority in the field of executive education and is much in-demand as a management consultant.

JOHN J. McDONOUGH is Associate Professor of Accounting and Information Systems at UCLA's Graduate School of Management. He received a bachelor's degree in economics from Dartmouth College and a master's degree and doctorate from Harvard University's Graduate School of Business Administration. His writings focus on issues of individual and organizational accountability in contemporary society. Dr. McDonough is active in professional and community affairs, serving as an Associate Editor of the *Journal of Applied Behavioral Science* and Chairman of the Los Angeles County Mental Health Commission.